The Great Tea Venture

Books by J. M. Scott

Heather Mary
The Man Who Made Wine
The Other Half of the Orange
Sea-Wyf
A Choice of Heaven
The Will and the Way
The Lady and the Corsair
The Great Tea Venture

J. M. SCOTT

The Great Tea Venture

ILLUSTRATED

New York: E. P. Dutton & Co., Inc.
1965

CONTENTS

ILLUSTRATIONS

ACKNOWLEDGEMENTS

To write a book is to make friends: it cannot be well done otherwise.

Since I first dipped into the story of tea my list of friends has steadily increased.

There are the historical characters, some of them authors, whom the reader will meet – Lu Yu, Howqua, Peter Mundy, Robert Fortune and others.

There are living authors of books on some aspect of tea-making and drinking who taught me most of what I know, among them those who very kindly gave me leave to quote from their works. These are included in the bibliography and in many cases also mentioned in the text. And there are those who provided the illustrations.

Finally, though their help in most cases was made available from the start, there are those who helped me with advice, introductions, suggested sources, or by correcting what I wrote.

Among these are Sir Percival Griffiths, President of the India, Pakistan and Burma Association and for many years adviser to the Indian Tea Association, and Miss Daphne Hammond, his secretary, the late G. H. Mardon, secretary until his death of the Indian Tea Association (London) and R. E. J. Hammond, his clerical assistant; also A. G. M. Morrison, President of the Tea Brokers Association and L. H. G. Gilbert of Messrs Ewart

Maccaughey; Cecil A. Crossle, C. J. E. Rathbone, Michael Adams, David Theobald and David Sykes of Messrs Lyons Tea Division; and D. M. Forrest of the Ceylon Tea Centre.

All these proved themselves good friends to me and to the book.

The Great Tea Venture

CHAPTER I

With hazard of all they had

Far in the dreamy East there grows a plant
Whose native home is the Sun's Cousin's garden.
Henrik Ibsen

ONE evening in the spring of the year 2737 B.C. the Emperor
Shen Nung was sitting before his camp-fire over which a cauldron of water was just coming to the boil. Shen Nung was
called the Divine Healer, and with good reason. The discovery
of the medicinal qualities of many herbs was ascribed to him.
He had ideas of hygiene far ahead of his time and he always
boiled his drinking water.

The fire crackled and hissed, for much of its fuel consisted
of branches broken from the camellia-like trees which grew
thereabouts.

Some scorched leaves swirled upwards in the column of hot
air, then slowly subsided. A good many fell into the pot. The
Emperor might well have thrown the water away, but the delightful scent now coming from the cauldron tempted him to
taste it. The flavour was astringent, clean, refreshing. As an
advocate of healthful concoctions it appealed strongly to him.
He began experimenting with more leaves of the same tree.

That is a free rendering of the Chinese legend about the
birth of tea. Dismiss it as a fairy story if you will, but admit that
a drink must be exceptional for people to have taken the trouble
to invent a story about its origin. I know of no other: even
wine just appeared – in time for Noah to get drunk on. But tea
has a pedigree and a worthy discoverer.

It is significant that the highly civilized Chinese who were soon looking upon tea as a special gift from heaven to them – and to them alone – should feel that no one less than a saintly emperor was worthy to have found it.

The Indians and the Japanese have different stories. In both cases the patriarch Darma, or Dharuma, was the discoverer. He devoted seven years to sleepless contemplation of the perfection of the Buddha, but during the fifth year began to feel sleepy. Struggling against this weakness of the flesh by every means he could he picked and chewed some leaves from a near-by bush – and, say the Indian Buddhists, immediately was once more in full command of all his senses. He had eaten tea-leaves! The Japanese story is the same as far as the onset of drowsiness. But their more drastic Darma cut off his eyelids and threw them away, and they sprouted up as tea plants.

The Chinese story is the best, and since in any case tea came from China let us work from that although we may not accept so precise a date for a prehistoric event.

Shen Nung is reported to have said, 'Tea is better than wine for it leadeth not to intoxication, neither does it cause a man to say foolish things and repent thereof in his sober moments. It is better than water for it does not carry disease; neither does it act like poison as water does when the wells contain foul and rotten matter.'

Tea is referred to here and there and more or less recognizably in Chinese writings throughout the early centuries of the Christian era. By the fifth century it had become an article of trade and a superlative growth from the Wen mountain was reserved for the Emperor as tribute tea.

The eighth century brought an event of great importance, the publication of the Tea classic, the *Ch'a Ching,* by Lu Yu. He is the first of the many interesting characters who pepper the history of tea. His work, part poetry, part etiquette-book and part text-book, had a very considerable effect at the time and also many centuries later.

He was a foundling, his finder a Buddhist priest who brought him up for the priesthood. But Lu Yu, whoever his parents may have been, was an individualist. He rebelled against the restrictions which the holy life involved. He was given menial tasks to teach him humility. He ran away.

He became a wandering clown. He was a great success, his

antics being greeted everywhere with roars of laughter. Yet he was sad at heart for he longed for knowledge. An official who admired him gave him books with which he educated himself. He became a scholar. Still he was not satisfied with life. There grew in him a yearning to pass on knowledge.

Tea by that time had ceased to be purely a medicine and become a pleasant drink, a social amenity. But knowledge of production methods was haphazard, disconnected, varying throughout the Empire. The tea merchants wanted it collected, sifted, put together in clearly understandable form.

Lu Yu did this, and more. Not only did he describe how tea was best grown, manufactured and infused. He also wrote of how it should be drunk – the ritual, the twenty-four instruments necessary for the tea equipage, for Chinese ceramic art was already well advanced. He was a master of simile. The best tea, he wrote, should 'curl like the dewlap of a bullock, crease like the boot of a Tartar horseman, unfold like mist rising out of a ravine, and soften gently like fine earth swept by rain'.

The *Ch'a Ching* – three volumes divided into ten parts – was published in A.D. 780. It brought to its author fame and fortune. The Emperor gave Lu Yu his patronage and friendship. He was revered by high and low. The tea merchants looked on him then, as they still do, as their patron saint.

But the man who was never contented refused to accept this adulation. What was fame? What were riches? What was the meaning of life? It was necessary to meditate on these profundities. He became a hermit, and as such he died.

What is most important to our story is that, for China, Lu Yu said the last word about tea. There was nothing to add. The right way to cultivate it, manufacture it, drink it had been laid down. There was nothing which the centuries could change. Tea was perfectly suited to the Confucian way of life – temperance, moderation, calm. It had become more than a national drink. Almost it was part of the religion of the people, a holy thing. The Chinese knew very little about the rest of the world, which must be composed, they believed, of races subject to themselves since their Emperor, the Son of Heaven, was Lord of everything under Heaven. They were the only civilization; the rest of the world was barbaric. They were entirely self-sufficient and supremely self-satisfied. At the time when the

Ch'a Ching was published they had every right to be, for China was undoubtedly the greatest civilization in the world.

II

When the *Ch'a Ching* was published Offa, who built the Dyke, was king of England – if England could then be considered a kingdom. King Alfred was a hundred years in the future and Magna Carta further still. Nearly six centuries were to pass before Chaucer became England's first poet. Whatever can be said of the English, they were a long way from being civilized.

Even 800 years later Queen Elizabeth was breakfasting on bread, flesh and a gallon of beer. Her subjects may not all have been so thirsty but they had no wider choice of beverages than she. It was 'feast on wine or fast on water'. Chiefly it was feast, for England had grown rich from her wool and powerful since her victory over maritime Spain. There was culture in the air – drama, music, poetry. There was ostentation too, a longing for luxury and novelty, pomp and pageantry. The Queen had a wardrobe of 3,000 costumes. The upper class created a demand for silks, brocades and velvets, for spices and exotic condiments to season food and drink.

To meet this demand there grew up a powerful middle class of tradesmen and merchants who sought the best means of procuring such luxuries from the Orient. Here England was at a disadvantage. Though Drake had sailed around the world she was not an ocean-going nation. Her little coastal ships had harried and broken the Armada. In international commerce Spain was still supreme in the West, Portugal in the East, with the Dutch following close upon their heels. When the Dutch and Portuguese combined to fix the prices the English merchants were in serious difficulties.

Elizabeth realized the importance of establishing direct trade relations with China. In 1596 she sent three ships commanded by Sir Robert Dudley with a letter to the Emperor. Nothing was ever heard of them again.

Undiscouraged by this the Queen looked favourably on an appeal by the London merchants to send trading fleets to the

4

Far East. In 1600 the Honourable East India Company, as it was later called, was inaugurated 'for the honour of the nation, the wealth of the people, the encouragement of enterprise, the increase of navigation, and the advancement of lawful traffic'. Elizabeth granted it a monopoly of all trade between the Cape of Good Hope and the Straits of Magellan.

This was a happening of the very greatest importance to this story, for the East India Company was to become far the biggest and most powerful monopolistic trading organization in tea – or in any other commodity – that the world has ever known. But that time was still the best part of a century ahead. Before reaching that chapter of events it is necessary to demonstrate the immense difficulty of establishing trade relations with China. Not until that was achieved could England receive tea in any quantity.

Tea had already been heard of in the West, but the descriptions did not make it possible to picture what it was like. In fact an English tea-drinker – had one existed – would scarcely have recognized it.

The first bold travellers among the xenophobic Chinese were Mohammedan traders and Jesuit missionaries. The first European reference to tea came as a quote from Hajji Mahommed in the second volume of Giambattista Ramusio's *Navigationi e Viaggi* published in Venice in 1559:

> 'They take of that herb, whether dry or fresh, and boil it well in water. One or two cups of this decoction taken on an empty stomach removes fever, headache, stomach-ache, pain in the side or in the joints, and it should be taken as hot as you can bear it. He said besides that it was good for no end of other ailments which he could not remember, but gout was one of them.'

The Jesuits praised tea for much the same reason that the Buddhist monks did, as a counter to alcohol. One recipe will serve as a fair example: 'To a pint of tea add the yolks of two fresh eggs; then beat them up with as much fine sugar as is sufficient to sweeten the tea, and stir well together. The water must remain no longer upon the tea than while you chant the Miserere psalm in leisurely fashion.' And then, presumably, you quickly got to heaven.

It was not specifically to procure this strange drink that

Englishmen tried to reach China. They could not be specific about anything since they knew so little about the products of the Orient. But of the general riches of Cathay they were certain, and it was this which drove them on, each year or decade a little farther. It was written:

> 'Concerning the Trade of China, three things are especially made known unto the world.
> 'The one is, the abundance of trade it affordeth.
> 'The second is, that they admit no stranger into their country.
> 'The third is, that Trade is as Life to the Vulgar, which in remote parts they will seek and accommodate, with hazard of all they have.'

At the birth of the seventeenth century, and of the Honourable East India Company, China seemed a very long way off. To reach the Americas was comparatively easy. They were much nearer and there was no land in the way. But sailing from England to China it was necessary to round the Southern Cape of Africa – a considerable voyage in itself – then cross the Indian Ocean, then find a way through a maze of uncharted rocks and islands. It was out of the question for the ships of the day to go so far without putting in once or twice for repairs and fresh stores. Therefore the object of the early voyages was to establish what amounted to advance bases.

Plans for the first voyage had been made by the East India merchants even before their charter had been granted by the Queen. On 13 February 1601 a fleet sailed under the command of Captain James Lancaster. There were five ships. The *Red Dragon*, the biggest, was of 600 tons, the smallest of 130 tons. The holds were full of stores, merchandise and gaudy gifts for native rulers, and on the decks were lashed 300 tons of cider and beer. The crews totalled 400 men.

The ships' stores were augmented when near the Canary Islands they overtook a Portuguese vessel loaded with wines, oil and fat. 'These', wrote the chronicler, 'were at once transferred to our ship and were of great help to us on the whole voyage thereafter.' Such acts were outlawed, but Lancaster carried an Ire (a right) of Reprisal. As no country nowadays ever commits atrocities in war, only reprisals, so it was then with piracy even in times of peace. Portugal at that time was under the Crown of Spain, and the ships of both countries were fair game for the English. It worked both ways, of course, depending on which side was stronger.

Even with this windfall Lancaster's stores ran low before he reached the Cape. He stripped his supply ship and set the empty hulk adrift. But a severe outbreak of scurvy forced him to put in to what is now Table Bay. It was the end of October before he sailed on, and not until June 1602 did he reach Achin on the north-west tip of Sumatra.

He was in no state to go farther east, into constricted seas which the Portuguese claimed as their own. But he came to a friendly arrangement with the fat and aged King of Achin who made him a present from his large stock of dancing girls. He had a certain amount of trade, put men ashore to start a 'factory' – the word means a complete trading establishment – office, store-rooms, living quarters. These were large and sturdy buildings, for in the early days they had sometimes to act as forts as well. The living quarters were often luxurious. Lancaster captured another rich prize before starting his homeward journey, which was to prove even more dangerous and difficult than the outward voyage. Such was overseas commerce at that time.

Lancaster returned to England to find that over 35,000 people had died of the plague in London out of a total population of not much more than 100,000. James I was on the throne of a united Scotland and England, a monarch who showed much less practical sympathy for merchant adventurers than had Elizabeth.

None the less the East India Company sent out four more ships in 1604 and three in 1607. Thereafter a voyage was made almost every year until 1615. By that date factories had been established at Surat and six other places in India, at Patani in Siam, at two places besides Achin in Sumatra, at Bantam and Jacatra in Java, at two places in Borneo, at Macassar and Banda in the Spice Islands and at Hirado in Japan. The merchant adventurers were closing in on China. But when, in 1617, King James attempted to send a letter to the Emperor he failed to have it delivered because, it was said, no Chinaman dared for his life to translate the letter, nor could any Christian be allowed to travel in China.

The first English trading venture forcefully pushed to a climax in China was not under the auspices of the East India Company. It was a piratical concern – not in the sense that its members were sea pirates, though they were not so far removed from that – but because by approaching China they contravened the royal charter of monopoly. That did not prevent Charles I, who had a quick eye for personal profit, from approving the venture and putting up £10,000. The affair is worth describing in some detail because it brought about the first encounter between the Chinese and English, and demonstrated the temperamental gulf between the world's two greatest tea-drinking nations – the age-old and the one which was yet to be.

Our chronicler is Peter Mundy, one of those immortals who do not feel they are living unless they are doing or seeing something unusual. He had to make a living, but he did not waste time earning more than necessary. What was essential was that he should travel, critically observe and minutely record in a diary which he must have spent most of his nights writing. (His spelling alone would make him worth quoting.) He had voyaged as a factor for the East India Company, made a land journey from Constantinople to London, conducted a caravan from Agra to Patna. He wrote that this sort of life had become 'somewhatt naturale unto mee'. In 1635, after spending as long a visit as he could stand to his family in Cornwall, he came to London and found himself the choice of two 'good businesses', one of them a voyage of 'unknowne designe'. This he chose.

The company planning the voyage was designated Courteen's Association. Its object was to set up trading centres in India and countries farther east, including China. The expedition consisted of four ships and two pinnaces and was commanded by Captain John Weddell. The chief merchant was Nathaniel Mountney. Peter Mundy signed on as a junior merchant.

Here we can only follow that part of the venture which concerns China. On 25 June 1637 what remained of Weddell's fleet – three ships and the pinnace *Anne* – dropped anchor off the Portuguese settlement of Macao.

The presence of foreign devils (as the Chinese called all

foreigners) not actually on the Chinese mainland but on a rocky peninsula off a deltaic island on the lower tip of Canton Bay, requires some explanation. Portugal had the biggest and briefest empire in history. After Bartholomew Diaz had reached the Cape of Good Hope, and Vasco da Gama had rounded it to reach India, the Portuguese Empire had rapidly spread its branches over the rich, virgin coasts and islands of the East. But it soon began to fade, insufficiently supported by its tiny root on the Iberian peninsula, while other trees with stronger roots began to overshadow it.

From 1517 until the middle of that century the Portuguese had maintained a buccaneering sort of commerce with several Chinese ports. Then the Celestials had taught them a sharp lesson, killing a good many and burning their factories. Thereafter they were restricted to Macao, a foot-shaped peninsula less than three miles long. Across the narrow, bony ankle, which the Chinese called the Stalk of the Lotus, was a high wall. Inside their concession the Portuguese had their own governor, senate and churches; and around the picturesque little harbour – in the instep of the foot – they built whitewashed dwelling houses in the same architectural style as those in their homeland. But the Chinese maintained their own officials as overlords. In fact they had these barbarians (what a name for the courteous, meticulous Portuguese!) exactly where they wanted them – right under their thumb. They could be trusted to behave and they provided a nice bit of revenue as duty on export goods sufficient to load one fleet a year for Japan and Manilla, and in consideration of the exclusion of all rival barbarians. Thus the Dutch were kept out of Macao, Canton and all the other ports of China although they were by then the strongest maritime nation. No doubt there was a good deal also to be paid out on the side, for officials have to live. But the Portuguese in this outpost were able to maintain, with cheap living conditions, the fine old form of life.

Into this little world sailed Captain John Weddell with the request that he should be assisted in trading with the Chinese. This blatant request, a demand in all but name, was based on a convention for truce and free trade recently signed at Goa, on the other side of India, from which Macao was effectively cut off by two Dutch fleets. There was also a letter from King

Charles. Weddell was a rough, tough sailor, very good at his job – trading and fighting were much the same – prepared to be patient and diplomatic to achieve his aim because so much money had been sunk in his venture, and in these oriental waters to which he was new he felt at the moment out of his depth.

He had the tact or caution to anchor three leagues outside the harbour of Macao, where even so he was immediately kept under surveillance by watch boats. Mountney, chief merchant, with Robinson and Mundy the two juniors, were sent ashore with the relevant letters to the Captain General of Macao.

Mundy's eyes were everywhere.

> 'Macao standeth at one end of a greatt
> Island built on rising hills, some gardains
> and trees among their houses making a
> pretty prospecte. . . .
> 'Many China vessells passing to and fro,
> none coming near us except the aforementioned
> watch boats.'

Domingos da Camara, Captain General of Macao, greeted the merchants 'with much respect and an answer promised the next day'. But this answer proved 'as false as prolix'. The gist of it was that the Portuguese would have liked to assist their English visitors but there simply was no trade to be got.

To prevent verification of this statement guard boats continued to keep Weddell's ship strictly segregated from any contact with the Chinese. Yet he was patient for he had been given a hint that once the Portuguese merchant ships then in the harbour had completed their loading for Japan he might expect better treatment.

He was not, however, a man to remain inactive for long, and after nearly three weeks of da Camara's politely vague promises he sent his pinnace, the *Anne*, to reconnoitre the approaches to Canton and try to establish direct trade with the Chinese.

This was done without reference to the Captain General. Canton was the true trading centre, a walled city of a million inhabitants – far bigger than the London of those days. The Portuguese themselves were excluded from it, except for a visit once a year to the trade fair. Since this great river-town and its approaches are the scene of much which is to follow it will be useful to describe the then uncharted waters which the *Anne* explored.

Canton Bay is funnel-shaped, about thirty miles deep and forty miles across. The thin, inland end of the funnel leads north to become the Pearl River. Macao is on the western extremity of the seaward opening. Crossing this opening eastwards one encounters the scattered Ladrones Islands, Lantao

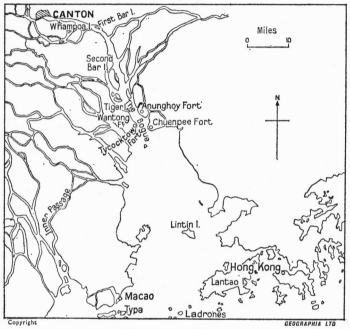

The Canton Estuary

Island and Hong Kong. Sailing up the bay one passes, right in the middle, Lintin Island, the Solitary Nail, 2,000 feet in altitude, in Weddell's day no more than a landmark and temporary anchorage but destined to become of great importance. As one sails farther up the bay the shores at last converge to form the Lion's Gate, the actual mouth of the Pearl River. This is the beginning of a defile six miles long and little more than a mile across in places, with steep hills on either side – narrow, wind-sheltered water, difficult to navigate even without opposition.

11

The Chinese had strengthened the Bogue, as the whole defile was called, with two forts on either side and a fifth on Tiger Island at its head.

Nature and the Chinese had thus made Canton impregnable to unwanted vessels – or so it would appear. Inland, for the remaining forty miles to the city, the Pearl is a meandering deltaic river with two shallow bars and numerous creeks and islands. Then one is suddenly inside China. The whole character of the countryside has changed. The hills are a vague mauve outline on the horizon. Foreground and middle distance form one vast rice plain. The wonderful green of rice, made still more vivid by the brilliant sun, is dotted with white pagodas and – if one could see clearly – tens of thousands of figures in blue smocks and trousers, the men only distinguishable by their pigtails, stooping over the muddy, timeless occupation of winning their daily food.

The *Anne* found her way to the Bogue, and a fisherman was bribed to guide her through. She got within fifteen miles of Canton. Then the authorities of the city, considerably disturbed by this penetration, stopped them by the simple method of promising them all the trade they wanted. The little ship sailed back to Macao to report.

Her arrival coincided with the departure of the Portuguese merchantmen for Japan. 'And now expected wee open admittance of trade.' But when nothing materialized Weddel decided to turn his back on Domingos da Camara, and with his four ships sailed into Canton Bay.

They were soon being shadowed by a fleet of war junks. Weddell was told to anchor and await permission from Canton. 'Howsoever that night we wayed and came further northward into the Bay.'

A few days later a force of forty junks, 'straunge vessells and as straungely fitted', repeated the order to go no farther. But Weddell, assuring them his object was only peaceful trade, which had already been promised, sailed through the Bogue as far as Anunghoy, the second fort on the right.

Here the Chinese showed signs of using force. Weddell, since his arrival at Macao, had often been in doubt about the right thing to do. But in these circumstances he acted instantly, ordering the waistcloths, a defence against boarders, to be mounted, downing the white ensign and the peaceful trading flag and running up in their places the Royal Arms and 'our bloudy ensign', the signal to engage.

At this the Chinese begged him to wait just six days more by which time the promised permission from Canton would *certainly* have arrived. They gave the English a white flag under the protection of which they were invited to go ashore and buy stores.

An uneasy peace lasted for three days. Then the English barge which had been sent to take soundings was fired on from the fort.

Weddell reacted at once. 'Outt went againe our Kings Coullours, wastclothes and bloudy ensign.' The four ships sailed up and anchored close in front of the formidable-looking fort.

The Chinese fired and the English replied – with this difference. The Chinese guns were fixed in their embrasures so that they shot as they pointed without the possibility of aim. Also their gunpowder must have been faulty, for some balls did little more than roll from the barrels, while the rest flew wide and far. Meanwhile the English shot with such speed and accuracy that within half an hour the defenders ran away. Thereupon a landing party replaced the Chinese flag with their own, took about forty guns, defaced the battlements and burned the interior. 'Herein, wee shewed our discontents for their refusing our friendly proffurs for a peaceful commerce.'

Shortly afterwards two junks and a fishing-boat were captured, and one of these vessels was sent up to Canton with a letter written in Chinese, 'Shewing therein a reason for our thus proceeding with them, and thatt contrariwise our desire was to have their Friendshipp and Free Commerce in their country.'

How this letter was translated is not stated. Interpreters were a problem, for no Chinese spoke English or Englishman Chinese. The best that could be hoped for was a half-breed who could render the local language into Portuguese. This difficulty remained until pidgin English was evolved.

But Weddell at this time was visited by a pretty fair example of the breed. He was a Chinese called Pablo Noretti, having acquired this name during a brief conversion to Christianity.

He came in the guise of a 'Petty Mandarine' with a message, he said, from the Great Mandarins of Canton who wished to know the grievances of the English. Weddell was assured of all the trade he wanted. It looked as if his forceful action had had a good effect.

Next day Noretti returned to Canton, accompanied by two of the English merchants. They were back within a week, the merchants pleasantly impressed by their courteous reception. Noretti brought a document in Chinese from the Tsungping, the Commander of the Green Banner troops of the Prefecture. This he translated as follows. The English would have free leave to buy and sell any commodity if they would pay the proper duties. Noretti should be their broker. Merchants should go to Canton to select goods, and the ships could have a choice of three places where to anchor. Finally it was politely requested that the guns and junks should be returned.

The Chinese document actually stated that the ships of the red-headed barbarians were to weigh anchor and sail out to sea immediately. They had no right whatever to come as they had without permission. It concluded, 'Should you have the great boldness to harm so much as a blade of grass or a piece of wood, I promise you that my soldiers shall make an end of you, and not a shred of your sails shall remain. You shall have no time for repentance and your sin shall not be forgiven.'

But Weddell did not know this. Acting on Noretti's rendering he did as he was asked, sending three merchants with a good supply of money, including 10,000 reals of eight as a present for the Mandarins. He did not realize that he was simultaneously defying a threat and giving hostages to the Chinese.

Soon after this he received a strong protest from the Portuguese at Macao, complaining about his interference with their trade and demanding that he should at once leave Chinese waters.

To this he answered:

'You appear to think that your letters, full of groundless threats, will induce us to abandon an undertaking so profitable and so certain. For which, though we pay no heed to your threats, we shall fight your people with blood and sweat to the end. This land, as you yourself acknowledge, is not yours, but the King of China's. Why then should we wait for licence from the King of Castille or his petty Viceroys in these parts?'

Further to encourage Weddell at this time he received from his merchants in Canton a load of sugar, the beginning of a cargo. He sent back a further 28,000 reals of eight.

The next move in this three-sided game came out of the darkness of a moonless night. As the tide was changing and the English vessels, anchored in the narrow waterway, were swinging slowly across the current three fire ships were sent against them. They drifted down with the ebb – tar, dry sticks and gunpowder blazing furiously, Greek fire, rockets and 'fire-arrowes' shooting out in all directions.

The English slipped or cut their cables, hoisted what sail they could and with the help of their ship's boats towing just got clear.

Weddell was shocked and angry. He hit out in all directions, burned several junks and a small town and blew up the fort. He furiously accused the Portuguese of complicity in the attack.

But after this outburst he woke up to realize his helplessness. Domingos da Camara denied any part in the affair. He was pained and surprised by such an accusation. The Chinese sent a gently worded note asking Weddell to wait patiently for *only ten days more*. Wait for what? He could not fight the whole of China. He was in narrow waters in which he could very easily be trapped. The information had been leaked that a powerful fleet was being prepared against him. Worst of all, his three merchants were being held in Canton in fear of their lives. They were allowed to write and say so.

He had got into a mess from which he could only extricate himself by climbing down. He was compelled to beg humbly of the Portuguese that they would intercede for him with the authorities of Canton. To the Chinese he equally humbly confessed his faults. Only then were his merchants released and was he permitted to leave with a small cargo of goods which he might have had with far less risk and trouble in India, Sumatra or Batavia. The exclusive growth of China was denied him as a piratical barbarian. The nearest thing to tea which he brought back was this description of it by Peter Mundy, whose book was widely read. Writing of the shopping party under the protection of a white flag on the shores of the Bogue he remarked on being given 'a certaine drinke called Chaa, which is only water with a kind of herbe boyled in itt. It must be dranke warme and is accompted wholesome.'

III

Weddell's venture did not bring trade with China – and therefore English tea-drinking – any nearer. His only achievement was to convince the Chinese that they had been right in their estimate of the Fan-Qui, the foreign devils. They were barbarians from beyond the pale of civilization. It was best to keep the door bolted while such people were about.

But the pressure of the expanding West – of its manufacturing and trading middle class – continued to increase. On the one hand there were more products in search of new markets; on the other, with the rising standard of living, there was a greater demand for Oriental luxuries, the more exotic the better. Consequently brave men in small, unhandy, square-rigged ships which were helpless in a storm and could not sail into the wind at all continued to hazard all they had on a round voyage of over 30,000 miles on the chance of being able to pick up a little trade from China. None succeeded by mere strength and courage. First they had to learn patience, apparent humility, and something of Confucian calm.

While they were painfully acquiring these some tea did get to Europe – not much, but enough to set people talking and wanting more. It did not come direct from China but was carried by Chinese trading junks to Java and Sumatra. There it was bought, especially by the Dutch, and brought to Europe. From Holland it was re-exported to France, and to England about 1670. The Portuguese in Macao sent it back to their homeland. It reached Russia by the overland route, which took eighteen months, quite early in the seventeenth century.

The first unquestionable reference to tea-drinking in England is in an announcement published by Thomas Garway in September 1658, and now in the British Museum:

'That excellent and by all Physicions approved drink called by the Chineans Tcha, by other nations Tay alias Tea is sold at the Sultaness Head a cophee house in Sweetings Rents by the Royal Exchange London.'

Tea was drunk in the coffee houses or taken home in jugs to be heated up at home. In 1660 it was taxed in liquid form at 8d a gallon and in 1670 at 2s a gallon. Samuel Pepys was referring to Coffee House tea when he wrote in his diary for 28 September 1660, 'I did send for a cup of tea (a China drink) of which I had never drank before.' Incidentally, this is the first reference to a Civil Servant drinking tea in his office.

The East India Company first imported tea (though still not direct from China) in 1664 – 2 lb 2 oz costing £4 15s with money worth about seven times as much as it is today. It was a present for King Charles. He possibly gave it to his wife, Catherine of Braganza who, being Portuguese, knew not only the drink but also the fashionable way of drinking it. To this she later introduced the ladies of her court. The East India Company gradually increased its imports. It could never at this time acquire much tea, for the supply brought in junks to the English factories of the Malay Archipelago was always small. In 1666 the Company bought 22 lb 12 oz for £56 17s 6d. In 1669 and 1670, in both cases from Bantam, they carried home 143 lb and 79 lb respectively. Thereafter almost every year for fifteen years they imported some tea from the same sources.

A great change took place in 1685. At last the ruling Chinese Emperor, K'Ang Hsi, relaxed his guard. He felt sufficiently sure of himself. Certainly Weddell and his like had proved how uncivilized and untrustworthy they were, but they had also shown that they were foolish people who could be dealt with effectively, and with a minimum of trouble provided they were kept on a short rein. They wanted to spend money. Why not let them? The Emperor decided to open all his ports under adequate safeguards to the Europeans. The duties demanded would be his private perquisite.

To this brief period of comparatively free trade belongs the first English import of tea direct from China – from Amoy in 1689. (Hence its name, t'e, pronounced tay, being the Amoy dialect word for tea. Ch'a is the Cantonese word.) Very soon the Emperor found it preferable to restrict all the trade to Canton. And there, officially at least, it remained for 160 years.

At first this trade was far from peaceful. Sometimes it was dangerous. In 1689 the *Defence*, a vessel of 700 tons, bound for Canton, was halted at Macao. One of her masts was towed a-shore and held as surety until all duties had been paid. These, when at last they had been fixed, amounted to £827 plus about £300 as a present to the chief customs officer. Captain Heath demurred, but was finally persuaded when the Chinese linguist begged that the payment should be made for otherwise he would be bambooed to death. So the captain met the charges and received a quittance, a chop as it was called. Then he sent his longboat ashore for the mast – only to find that it was being held by the military to whom the customs officer's quittance meant nothing. In other words a further payment was expected.

The English sailors thereupon took the mast by force and made it fast behind the longboat preparatory to towing it out to the ship. There was a scrimmage at the water's edge. 'When,' states a contemporary account, 'began the enemies to pour whole showers of stones at our boats; our people not enduring the onsett desired leave to fire . . . The word "fire" it seems was fatally given by the captain and upon't two or three of the people fired immediately, killing one and wounding another Chinaman on the spot; on which our boat putt off in confusion.'

A Chinese vessel returned the fire, wounding the pilot who stood at the captain's side. The mast was cut loose, and the longboat pulled away, leaving behind on the shore the doctor, the mate and seven sailors. These were cut down in sight of their companions.

It was an ugly affair, discreditable to both sides. The East India Company was much concerned that all trade might be cancelled. Instead it was allowed to continue – on Chinese terms, and at Canton only.

The conditions under which Europeans were allowed to trade at Canton were called the Eight Regulations and were briefly as follows. No war vessel could come up the Pearl River and no arms might be brought in. The merchant ships must anchor at Whampoa, thirteen miles below Canton, and do their loading and unloading there. The business houses could set up factories in a specified area outside the walled city, but

18

Processes of Chinese tea manufacture

The Grand Hoppo is entertained by the British merchants at Canton

Europeans might only live there during the winter, and then without their wives. Strict restrictions were placed upon their movements, recreations and servants. They were not to mix with the public and must do all business with the officially appointed Canton monopoly known as the Co-Hong. All complaints or petitions to higher authority must be passed through this body.

In other words foreigners were controlled both in their public and private lives, and the only body to whom they might make representations had neither authority to meet complaints nor advantage in forwarding them.

The Emperor wanted the maximum profit and the minimum trouble. Granted that as the object, it is difficult to imagine a sounder or more logical system. The Emperor appointed an officer to collect for him what may be very loosely described as the trading duties. His title was Hai Kwan Pu – which the British quickly corrupted to Hoppo. The Hoppo's duty was to transmit to the Emperor a sum dependent on the tonnage of foreign ships in port. He received no salary from the Emperor for this work. He bought the appointment. Under the Chinese system the employee paid the employer. The Hoppo got his salary from the Hong merchants whom he appointed. There were about eight of them. Their *minimum* yearly payments for the privilege of being thus employed were calculated by Dr Morrison, the East India Company's interpreter, to be as follows: presents for the Emperor on his birthday and on other occasions, £56,000; presents direct to the Hoppo, £14,000; tips to other officials, £14,000; the Yellow River Fund (officially a charity, but one which not only began but ended in the Hoppo's home), £10,000; compulsory purchase of Ginseng (a medicinal root), £46,000. This adds up to £140,000 which these eight men had to pay to their employer yearly.

It was a heavy burden. Occasionally one went bankrupt and could not meet his commitments to the barbarians. To guard against this embarrassing possibility a sort of insurance fund was started. It was called the Consoo Fund and consisted of an *ad valorem* charge of three to six per cent on all goods which passed through the customs. This was paid, of course, by the barbarians and amounted to £2,300,000 a year. By 1841 when it was last – and most appropriately – used it still ran into millions.

The disciplinary system was no less sound. The Hoppo was responsible to the Emperor for anything which might go wrong. He made one of the Hong merchants responsible for each ship in port. The merchant had no authority, of course, but he could be much more easily and safely punished than the foreigners – the customers. Also, the fact that an innocent man was suffering for their offences did for some reason help to keep the barbarians in order. As a last resort trade could be stopped. It was so simple.

The Hong members were also personally responsible for the behaviour of individual merchants. Again they had no authority. To prevent their often unruly charges from getting them into trouble they had to depend on links of friendship, on charm and tact. The following letter is an example. (The name of the addressee is a Chinese attempt at a European pronunciation, and the mention of age is a term of respect.)

> 'Ham Tak, venerable old gentleman – we beg respectfully to inform you that we have heard of the intention of our respected elder brother and other chin-te-le-mun (gentlemen) to race boats on the river. We know not if this is true, but heretofore it has not been custom. Should the authorities hear of this, we your younger brothers would be reproved, not mildly, for permitting you to act so indiscreetly. On the river, boats are mysteriously abundant; everywhere they congregate in vast numbers; like a stream they advance and retire unceasingly. Thus the chances of contact are many, so are accidents, even to the breaking of one another's boats, to the injury of men's bodies, while more serious consequences might ensue.
>
> 'We therefore beseech our worthy senior to make known to the other chin-te-le-mun that they would do well to refrain from contesting the speed of their boats on the river, so that after troubles should not accumulate. Then all will be well. Daily may your prosperity increase, without difference.'

Who could resist that sort of thing? The system worked.

Chinese was an extremely difficult language for a foreigner to learn, the more so since Chinese teachers were liable to be decapitated and therefore had to give lessons in the strictest secrecy. Officially the merchants talked and wrote only through an official interpreter, a 'linguist'. Personal contact was frowned upon by the Chinese autocracy, even to that extent. (Anyone who, like myself, has tried to work in a Communist country sees a parallel today.) Thus, since men must talk face to face to do business efficiently, a *lingua franca* was evolved. Pidgin or pigeon (one finds both spellings for this phonetic language) is, one is told, a corruption of the word 'business'. It sounds thoroughly corrupted, but at any rate that is the meaning. Pidgin English is business English. There is no grammar. Chinese, Portuguese, Indian and English words, pronounced as a Chinese hears them, are the constituents. For instance mandarin comes from the Portuguese *mandar*, to order – and means any official, any civil servant. Compradore comes from *compra*, to buy, joss from *dios* – thus joss house, temple. Coolie and chit are of Indian origin. English words are numerous and generally recognizable. The result is a comic sort of baby talk in which it is practically impossible to be serious. In the early days this matched the point of view of the foreign chin-te-le-mun trading in China. The Chinese were aggravating but individually likeable children. Now, probably without realizing it, we still use a few pidgin words and phrases – chin-chin, a Chinese greeting between equals, 'Hai, chin-chin' meaning 'How are you, Hail, hail!' and 'It's not my pidgin', not my business.

The Chinese names for the different nationalities are interesting. All foreigners were barbarians or Fan-qui. But the British were red-haired devils, a distinction which one guesses was suggested by temperament as well as colour, in which it is scarcely accurate. The Parsees with their shaven pates were white-headed devils. Negroes, Moors, were molo devils, Americans flowery-flag devils, and the Portuguese Macao devils.

Reference has been made to the trading duties. A better phrase might be money directly demanded. This varied – there was never a fixed rule, for it depended on how much they thought they could get. But a fair example is that a ship had to pay 2,000 taels – £650 – in presents for a start, then a tax which depended on her length and beam, and finally up to fifteen per cent of the value of the cargo with the Consoo Fund contribution on top of that. Only when these had been handed over was the Grand Chop issued, permitting her to sail. These were basic charges. If anything out of the ordinary were required, or some quite ordinary thing were wanted quickly, more grease was needed before the complex machinery began to work.

Time was the only thing of which the Chinese were prodigal. They let it flow. But it was vital to a ship's captain who must get away with the north-east monsoon or waste a season. A common practice of an insufficiently lubricated Hoppo was to refuse to measure a ship, which meant that trading could not even begin. But the most interesting thing about the whole business is that everyone made money. Occasionally, as has been said, a Hong merchant was squeezed to bankruptcy by the Hoppo, and the Consoo Fund (barbarian money) had to be used to liquidate his debts. But one Hong merchant at least was said to be worth £5,000,000 sterling. The Hoppo must have been proportionately richer. This suggests fantastic fortunes. And yet the barbarians from whom all this money ultimately came also grew richer. The East India Company, which by its monopoly was the only English company permitted to trade in China, and which soon became the biggest trading organization of any nationality, steadily increased its profits. That gives an idea of the value of the China trade.

At first the commodity chiefly sought after was silk. But tea soon superseded it. The goods which the English mainly offered in return were British broadcloths, which were not much wanted in semi-tropical Canton. Rarely could we obtain more than a third of the tea we required by barter. The rest had to be paid for in silver.

The actual business was done by the Hong merchants on the Chinese side and the supercargoes, the ships' merchants, on the other. The supercargoes of the East India Company were re-markable men. In a country full of experts in silk they had to be able to assess at a glance the value of the sample offered, and they had to know all about the numerous types of tea. Each had to be recognized and its current value known.

The adverse balance, as has been said, was paid in silver. But it was illegal to export English silver coins. So the currencies which the supercargoes dealt in were Spanish reals of eight, and pillar dollars (which carried a design of the Pillars of Hercules), Mexican dollars, ducats from Venice, French crowns, rix dollars – each of which had a different value.

But far more serious than difficulties of calculation was the fact that the English merchants had to buy two-thirds of the tea for hard cash brought out from England because the Hong merchants in Canton were not much interested in the goods they had to offer, and by the regulations they were not allowed to offer them anywhere else in the whole vast empire of China which reached from the tropics to the bitterly cold north, where woollen cloth might have been welcome. It was a situation to drive any salesman mad.

At the beginning the adverse balance was not very large for by the year 1725 England had only imported a *total* of 250,000 lb of tea. But eighty years later British imports were *averaging* 24,000,000 lb, most of it bought for silver. It would seem that the drain on British currency must soon have become economically unsupportable. Yet these conditions remained until the middle of the nineteenth century, which at this stage of the story was still a long way off.

CHAPTER II

Production in China

What tongue can tell the various kinds of tea?
Of Blacks and Greens, of Hyson and Bohea,
With simple Congou, Pekoe and Souchong,
Cowslip the fragrant, Gunpower the strong?

Anon

BY the middle of the eighteenth century the European merchants in Canton were competent tea buyers. They could
recognize the different types and judge their value. Modern
descriptions would be confusing, but the types then in vogue
are listed here with a brief description of each, taken from a
booklet of the period.

'Black Teas:

'Bohea – Is of a black cast, and yields a deep yellowish infusion;
sells in China for twelve to fifteen tales per pecul. (A tale was
worth 6s 8d – a third of a pound sterling – and a pecul was
133 lb 5 oz. The sum need not be worked out, but by including
these prices the relative value of the teas can be seen.) The strength
of Bohea is drawn out quickly.

'Sometimes it has a faint smell not unlike that of dried hay.
When put in water it produces a colour of the deepest tincture,
resembling mahogany or an infusion of tobacco, a colour much
disliked by all judges of tea.

'Congou – The infusion is lighter than that of Bohea, rather
green. When put into water it should produce a colour resembling
pale amber; but it is often mixed with Bohea, and then it produces a high colour. The taste of Bohea, however, always pre-
dominates. Sells for twenty-five to twenty-seven tales per pecul.
Congou will bear three waters.

'Souchong – The leaves are long and slender, but with a crispness that is not to be met with in any other quality, and on putting a little in the mouth it causes an agreeable roughness. The smell is very sweet notwithstanding it causes a sensation of an agreeable acid. In water it produces a liquor of light amber colour. Sells for forty to fifty tales per pecul.

'Pekoe – This is the superior quality of black tea. The appearance is almost jet black. Pekoe is considered to be the first shoot of the plant, which produces the flower. It has a most delicate and pleasant smell, rather faint and not unlike that of cowslips. When in water it produces a pale liquid. This tea is not agreeable to many palates of itself, but to improve other teas it is of inestimable value. Sells for thirty-four to sixty tales per pecul. Pekoe creams briskly when poured out. The water must stand on it a considerable time to draw its virtue, and it will draw four or five waters.

'Green Teas:

'Singlo and Twankay – The leaf is small and light curled at the end. The smell is very refreshing and it is a good and wholesome tea. Sells for twenty-four to twenty-six tales a pecul. It will bear three waters well.

'Hyson – so called from a Mr Hyson, a rich East India merchant who first imported it. Hyson has a smaller, harder and more curled leaf. It is of a blue colour, nearly resembling the bloom of a sloe, very fragrant to smell and heavy in the hand. It also tastes crisp in the mouth when chewed. When made into tea it scarcely tinctures the water. To ascertain if Hyson be good let a cup of its liquor stand all night, then if its colour, delicate smell and bitterish taste continue, it is good. But if these be impaired it is old and has lost part of its virtue. Sells for fifty to sixty tales per pecul. Young Hyson will bear four waters.

'Gunpowder – The leaf of this tea is much smaller, being only about twice as large as a middling grain of gunpowder. It is the strongest green tea imported. It will draw four or five waters.'

That, very briefly, is what the merchants of the eighteenth century knew of the teas they bought. Since the gardens were far from Canton, in the prohibited interior of China, they knew nothing at first hand about the growing of the bushes and the manufacture of the leaves. The strip cartoon which faces p. 6 represents all they were able to learn from the Chinese merchants.

(1) 'The first process is that of making holes in the ground, at short distances from each other, and in a straight line. This is done by labourers, with an implement for the purpose with a long handle and sharp-pointed head.

'After the ground is prepared, another class of labourers is employed in sowing the seed. This is done by putting a few of the seeds, varying in number from six to twelve, into each of the holes, which are generally four or five inches deep in the ground; they are then watered, and they vegetate with little more care.

(2) 'As the plant grows, it requires occasional watering; and careful persons are employed to enrich the ground by a mixture of soil and manure.

'The next part of the process is that of gathering the leaves, which is not done until the Tea-Plant has reached three years' growth; they are then very carefully plucked, one by one, lest the branches of the Plant should be torn, or the leaves injured. And here we may be permitted to remark, that nothing can more clearly point out the unremitting labour and industry of the Chinese, than the preparation of this Plant for the market; and it is a curious circumstance, that a body of merchants in England should furnish employment to more than a million of the subjects of a nation that despises those merchants, and throws every obstacle in the way of commercial intercourse.

(3) 'When the leaves have been gathered, they are sorted into classes, according to their size and quality, previous to their being dried; and care must be taken that there are not too many in one heap, or they will get spoiled.

'The methods of preparing the leaves of Tea, are nearly the same both by the Japanese and Chinese, the only difference appearing to be, that the latter expose the leaves to the steam of boiling water, or put them in hot water, for half a minute, a process not observed by the Japanese.

'Kœmpfer, who is the most minute as well as the most accurate in his details, informs us that the Tea leaves, when gathered, are prepared in the Tsiusi, as they are called, that is public drying-houses or laboratories built for the purpose and where every person may bring leaves to be dried; for many are either ignorant of the manner of preparing them or have not the necessary apparatus. There are in these public laboratories:

'(i) Several ovens, sometimes as many as twenty, each of which are three feet high, with a wide, flat, square or round iron pan at the top; the side, over the mouth of the oven, is bent upwards for the person who attends the drying, who stands on the opposite side secure from the fire and turns the leaves.

'(ii) One or more low but very long tables, covered with fine reed mats on which the leaves are to be rolled.

'(iii) A number of workmen, some of whom are employed in attending the drying of the leaves in the open, and others sitting cross-legged by the tables to roll the leaves as they come hot from the pan.

'The leaves must be dried when fresh; and they are generally brought to the laboratory the same day they are gathered. The process of drying is thus performed:

'Some pounds of the leaves are put into the iron pan, which by the fire underneath has already been heated to that degree that the leaves when they are put in may crackle at the edges of the pan. The fire in the oven must also be so regulated that the man attending the drying-pan may be able to stir up the leaves with his hands, which he continues to do until they become so hot that he cannot handle them any longer: the instant they become so he takes them out of the pan with a shovel, broad at the mouth like a fan, and pours them upon the mat in order to be rolled.

(4) 'Each person takes before him a quantity of the leaves and, whilst they are hot, immediately commences rolling them in the palms of his hands, until they are cold, by which means they are equally curled.

'When thus curled, they are again delivered to undergo a second drying over the fire in the pans, until they have given out all their juice. In this second drying they are stirred, not quickly and hastily as in the first, but very slowly and deliberately for fear of breaking the curls. After this second drying they are again delivered to the rollers, who roll them a second time in the same manner; and if the leaves are not fully dry the process of drying and rolling is repeated a third time.

'Great care is taken in the second and third drying that the heat of the fire be lessened in proportion as the leaves have lost their juices and humidity, or they would be burnt or turned black. For the more valuable Teas the drying and rolling are repeated four or five and even seven times, thus drying the leaves more gradually, by which means they preserve that lively and agreeable green colour which distinguishes the best Teas. The pans are always washed clean with hot water between each drying because a sharp juice sticks to the edges and bottom of the pan, which is apt to discolour the leaves.

'The drying and curling of the leaves being finished they are spread on the floor or on tables covered with mats and are sorted into classes, by which the grosser leaves and such as are not well curled or too much burnt, are separated from the rest. The dust and smaller leaves are also separated by means of sieves.

(5) 'When the Tea has been dried, it is packed in earthen vessels or baskets; and after it has been kept for some months in these it is taken out and again dried over a very gentle fire in order to deprive it of any humidity it might still have retained or contracted during the rainy season.

(6) 'The Tea is preserved from the air in earthen or porcelain vessels until it is packed into boxes lined with lead, covered with a species of fine tissue paper, in which manner it is exported.

'The Chinese preserve the finest sorts of Tea in conic vessels, like sugar loaves, made of tutenague, tin, or lead, covered with neat matting of bamboo, until packed for exportation.'

CHAPTER III

Smuggling

I like a smuggler. He is the only honest thief.
He robs nothing but the revenue – an abstrac-
tion I never greatly cared about. I could go out
with him in his mackerel boat, or about his less
ostensible business, with some satisfaction.

Charles Lamb

Smuggler – A wretch who, in defiance of justice and the laws, imports or exports goods
either contraband or without payment of the
customs.

Dr Johnson's Dictionary

WHEN tea came to England in the late seventeenth century,
and for at least a hundred years thereafter, inland communications were by present standards almost unimaginably bad.
Most roads were tracks, dangerous at night. The country was
made up of market towns and their villages, forming self-sufficient groups. Most people lived and died within ten or twenty
miles of where they were born, and neither knew nor cared
what was happening in the rest of the land. Being for the most
part illiterate they could not read about it.

Hardly the situation for a nation-wide sales campaign of an
expensive novelty. Yet in this period tea became the national
drink, replacing ale at breakfast and closing down the gin houses
where one was invited to get drunk for a penny and dead drunk
for twopence.

This could not in the first instance have been due to tea's
essential virtue, for how could common people even taste it?

29

Rather it was brought about by the propensity tea has – or at least had – of being associated with trouble.

Good tea at first cost at least 60s a pound. The cheapest sort one could legally buy cost 7s – nearly as much as a labourer could earn in a week. But the same quality was available on the Continent – just across the Channel or the North Sea – for 2s a pound and inferior sorts for much less. The reason was that the Revenue authorities had in 1680 slapped on a duty of 5s a pound irrespective of quality. For the more expensive teas this made comparatively little difference. But it appeared to knock cheap tea right out of the market.

Not the black market, though. The free traders, as they called themselves, had a profit of 350 per cent to play with, and they were not slow to start the game. The trouble and talk which resulted publicized tea as nothing else could have done, and as the illegal industry spread and prospered it carried the new commodity to every door. It was calculated that at the height of this illegal campaign two-thirds of the tea drunk in England had been smuggled.

An efficient free trading organization already existed – and a preventive system which was both inefficient and inadequate. Large-scale smuggling had started 200 years earlier with the export of wool. (In those days it was bad economics and therefore largely forbidden to export a country's most valuable goods.) The smugglers had later turned their attention to the import of silk, lace, spirits, tobacco and an ever-growing list of dutiable commodities. For them tea was a natural. Sewn up in canvas bags it was easily handled and hidden and was safe from damage. Pounds of it could be carried in the lining of specially made clothes. Once inside the country it was impossible to tell before the days of packaging whether a quantity of tea had paid duty or not. And the big margin of profit meant that even if two runs in three were lost the smugglers were still in pocket.

In fact they hardly ever lost a run. Their organization was briefly as follows. The capital was put up by the Venturer who adventured only financially, keeping well in the background. Many of the fine old houses near our coasts were built with the fortunes that these people made. The Captain and the Lander took the risks. The Captain carried the investment over to

France, Holland or the Channel Islands, which were free of customs control. There he made his purchase legally. So far his only fault lay in taking money out of the country. He waited for a suitable night to run the goods across the Channel to one of several alternative landing places. This was arranged with the Lander, who laid on the porterage, storage and distribution arrangements. These three men, with the Quill Driver who kept the accounts – very possibly the only person besides the Venturer who could read and write – were the individuals chiefly engaged.

The lesser fry were, under the Captain, fishermen for whom this was a far more paying enterprise than fishing, and one moreover which they could practise under that guise. The Lander could get all the porterage he wanted from among the farm labourers of the district. Living was expensive, wages were low, and a man could make more by carrying goods for one night than he could by working in the fields for a week.

For the run, alternative nights were selected during the 'darks', when the moon was small. On the first on which the weather served the Captain crossed the Channel. Approaching the English coast he made a signal – a coloured light, perhaps. In answer a light which shone through a tapering tube was aimed at him. It was moved or otherwise manipulated to show that the coast was clear (one notices a common phrase in its original, literal sense). If the coast was not clear of preventive officers the Captain made for an alternative rendezvous or turned back and tried again later.

Variety is the essence of successfully fooling the law, and there were besides completely different methods of getting the stuff in. For instance, fishing smacks put out from their home port with their usual small crew and nothing except fishing gear aboard. Out at sea they were met by a number of small craft with more men, merchandise and money. Thus fully equipped they crossed to the Continent, bought what they wanted, and recrossed the Channel or North Sea in the night. By using light signals they once more gathered their fleet of little boats. These took off the extra men and contraband while the smacks sailed back to their home port as apparently innocent as they had set out.

Small boats could be beached, which made unloading easier, and could run in almost anywhere along the coast. Some made the whole crossing from France or the Channel Islands direct, without depending on any parent ship. The bold and skilful Cornishmen favoured this method. Others met foreign ships at sea, and others – at a later date – the big East Indiamen returning from China. In recorded instances the offices of the Honourable Company sold tea over the side in view of a revenue cutter but outside territorial waters. Lastly, in this list of specimen methods, there was smuggling by concealment in cross-channel cargo vessels engaged in otherwise legitimate trade. Against so many and so varied methods the defence had their work cut out.

Imagine a game with rules which were restrictive only for one side. The forces were far from equal. The smugglers could have as many men as they wanted. Almost everyone was on their side, played for it professionally when they could, backed it for the advantage they got out of it or from timidity kept silent about its activities. The preventive team was limited in numbers and enterprise, on the one hand by the parsimony of the official purse and on the other hand by fear. They had good reason to fear reprisals.

In 1703 a Riding Officer, the current term for a preventive man on land, got £60 a year, plus an allowance of £30 for a servant and a horse to assist him during the night. Those who took this employment had the choice of being lax and collaborating, or of being dutiful at the risk of getting their throats cut or being kidnapped, carried out to sea and dumped over the side, well ballasted with stones. Officially the Riding Officers could call for assistance from the Dragoons, but there had been arguments over sharing prizes and the military were slow to get moving when alerted. Besides, they objected to marching any distance. There were fifty Riding Officers for most of the coastline of Kent and Sussex, a stretch of about 200 miles. There is no record of how many smugglers used this stretch, but it must have been many hundreds, if not thousands.

At sea there were the revenue sloops and cutters which were assigned to guard particular areas. They were inadequate in number, their crews too often lazy or timid and generally jealous of the men on land rather than co-operative. The best that can be said of this period is that it was the beginning of yacht racing – revenue cutters chasing smugglers who almost invariably won the cup of tea. It was not fair sport. The races started at a time and place chosen by one side, in the greatest secrecy, so generally there was no revenue yacht on the starting line, the limit of territorial waters.

The smugglers, with the whole countryside sympathetic to them, had an excellent intelligence system. They knew when a revenue cutter was hauled out of the water to have her bottom scraped, when a Riding Officer had gout or a plan of interception was afoot. The preventive men on the other hand were treated like an enemy of occupation and could learn nothing true from the locals.

This general sympathy for the free traders was the most important factor in the struggle. Not only would nobody inform against them, but farms with their barns and haystacks, even churches with their crypts and tombs made excellent caches. Tea and tobacco were such harmless things. As for brandy, if the Government had to have taxes why couldn't they tax something else? Sometimes it went much further than that, for comparatively few people saw anything wrong in the killing of a customs officer. It might be dangerous but the excise man deserved his fate for not taking the bribe which was always available and letting folk have a few amenities at prices they could afford.

This point of view is brought out by the Rev. R. S. Hawker of Morwenstow on the Cornish coast. He was a vicar of the real old school, cultured, broad-minded, active, put out by nothing – shipwreck, violent death or the most outrageous opinions. Two of the stories he tells come from his oldest parishioner and take us back to the period being described.

'Ah! He was a dear old man our parson, mild as milk; nothing ever put him out. Once I mind, in the middle of morning prayer, there was a buzz down by the porch, and the folks began to get up and go out of the church one by one. At last there was hardly three left. So the parson shut the book and took off his surplice and said to the clerk: "There is surely something amiss." And so there certainly was; for when we came out on the cliff there was a King's cutter in chase of our vessel, the *Black Prince*, close under the land and there was our departed congregation looking on. Well, at last Whorwell, who commanded our trader, ran for the gullrock (where it was certain death for anything to follow him), and the revenue commander sheered away to save his ship. Then off went our hats, and we gave Whorwell three cheers. So, when there was a little peace, the parson said to us all, "And now, my friends, let us return and proceed with divine service." We did return; and it was surprising after all the bustle and uproar, to hear how parson Trenworth went on just as nothing had come to pass: "Here beginneth the Second Lesson . . . ."'

The second story is of this same priest presiding – white-haired, benign, patriarchal – at a village feast. There was much whispering, and the prompting of a spokesman among the farmers at the lower end of the table. At last it came out, they wanted to know if there were an unforgivable sin. Shocked and surprised the parson answered that he trusted there was none to which they might be liable. What were they thinking of? 'Why, sir,' said the spokesman, 'we thought that if a man should find out where run goods was deposited and should inform the gauger (the revenue man), that such a villain was too bad for mercy.'

Smuggling, with popular sympathy for the free trader, was not confined to the southern counties. All the way up both the east and west coasts goods were run.

East Anglia was not behindhand. Lord Teignmouth tells that at 2 o'clock one morning two men arrived at Hythe quay near Colchester. They said they were revenue officers and wished to lodge some captured goods in the Customs House. The Customs House was opened to them – and from close behind them out of the night there entered thirty smugglers armed with blunderbuss and pistol, blacksmith's hammers and crowbars. Nobody interfered with them, and they went away with 1,514 lb of tea.

A trouble on the east coast was the extent of sandy flats on which the feet of laden men left tracks which were easy to read and follow. But for a consideration the local shepherd would drive his flock over the sand directly the gang had passed.

Scotland did not lag behind. Her people were even less sympathetic towards customs officers than they might have been, since Parliament was trying to unite the revenue systems of Scotland and England, much against Scottish will.

Such was the popular mood when two smugglers, Wilson and Robertson, were arrested and condemned in 1736. They made an early attempt to escape from the Tolbooth in Edinburgh where they were confined. But Wilson, a herculean giant, stuck in the small window, bottling up his companion until the guards appeared. He was deeply ashamed of this 'and determined to make up for it.

On the Sunday before their execution they were taken to church. Soon after the service started Wilson grasped his companion by the belt and hurled him clear of their guards. Before they could react he had, in the words of the poet Allen Ramsay:

'A soldier held fast with each hand and one of them with his teeth, while Robertson got over and through the pews, pushed o'er the elder and plate at the door, made his way through the Parliament Close, down the back stair, got out of the Poterow Port before it was shut, the mob making way and assisting him, got friends, money and a swift horse and fairly got off, nae mair to be heard of or seen.'

When Wilson came to be executed the populace showed their sympathy for him by turning out in enormous numbers. Children in those days could be trusted to find their own amusements, and a number of boys were in the crowd to watch the hanging. Afterward they threw stones at the executioner. They were not large stones, nor were they accurately thrown. But Captain Porteous, in charge of the city guard, was in a nervous state. He fired into the crowd and ordered his men to do the same. The crowd scattered, leaving three men, a boy and a woman dead. Porteous ordered another volley which killed two more youths and a tailor in a third-storey window. There were a good many wounded.

Porteous was locked up. But the Law was uncertain what to do with him. The citizens of Edinburgh settled it by breaking into the jail, dragging out Porteous and stringing him up on a lamp post. He was 'nane the waur o' a hanging', they thought. Westminster did not agree. The Lord Advocate, Duncan Forbes, who will be heard of later for his views about tea, had to fight hard to water down legal reprisals against the city of Edinburgh.

The Isle of Man was so great an entrepôt for smuggled goods

that it deserves to be introduced with a few sentences of history. The Welsh kings ruled the island until near the end of the ninth century when the Scandinavians took it over. In 1266 King Magnus of Norway ceded his rights to it and the Hebrides to Alexander III of Scotland. On his death the Manx people placed themselves under the protection of Edward I of England. In 1406 the island was given to the Stanley family in perpetuity, under the English crown. They ruled it, latterly as 'Lords', until a death without direct issue in 1735, when it passed to the Dukes of Athol who held by charter the royalty giving exemption from duty on a number of importations. Thus, with little sense of responsibility to the English crown, the Isle of Man began a smuggling spree. Offering freedom from duty it attracted cargoes which would otherwise have been delivered to Liverpool or Bristol, and its sailors later ran the goods on to the Galloway or Cumberland coasts. The whole countryside was in the racket, from the cottager to the prosperous farmer, the laird, the parson. The country people dealt with smugglers not only for the sake of getting luxuries cheap, but of getting them at all. On the lonely Mull of Galloway, in parts of which until quite recently the nearest post office was in Ireland, it was not possible to purchase legally such amenities as brandy, tobacco and tea. Smugglers were the only tradesmen who delivered to the door – or rather to the unshuttered window, with a masonic tap-tap-tap at dead of night.

Robert Burns's 'The Diel's awa' wi' the Exciseman' was inspired on that coast. Sir Walter Scott's Dick Hatteraick was the Dutchman Yawkins who bore down on two converging revenue cutters, passing so close to both that he threw his hat on the deck of one and his wig on the other. That sort of story was repeated with pride, to the advantage of the smugglers' reputations. One parson preached seventeen times on the text 'Render unto Caesar —', but he persuaded no one to render revenue unto the crown. Almost everyone had a secret hole, under the farm kiln, under the sitting-room fireplace, or under the dining-room table, a trap-door covered by the carpet. Quite recently a horse and cart fell through the roof of a hiding-place, and rootling pigs discovered another.

To show what happened when the excisemen interfered I quote from a local newspaper of 1771.

'On Thursday last at midday, in contempt of the authorities, civil and military, there marched through the parish in the direction of Dolmillington upwards of one hundred smugglers, with about one hundred and fifty horses, all laden with tea, tobacco and spirits. They were laden at the Bay of Luce in Galloway from three luggers from the Isle of Man: there were about two hundred of the smugglers there, but the rest took another road, and the vessels being disturbed sailed for the coast of Ireland to discharge the rest of their cargoes. The band which passed through this place had been attacked by a party of military and excise officers; but the soldiers, consisting of a Sarjeant and sixteen men, were defeated, got their firelocks broke, and several of them nearly killed.'

There is also a romantic story of a troop of horses, their flanks well greased, and carrying nothing except a loosely slung load of contraband, which galloped through the night from the landing cove led by a mare which knew the way to the inland hide-out on the moors. Picture such a ghostly cavalcade. Imagine the stories which would be told about it.

From other sources come two tales, one actually of a revenue man's success. Patrolling by night below Birling Gap in Sussex he stumbled upon a group of smugglers, who ran. Groping about in the dark he found a load attached to a rope. He gave this a pull. It was suspended from a derrick by means of which another party 300 feet above was engaged in getting the contraband up the cliff, and a pull on the rope was the signal to hoist. Before he knew what was happening the revenue officer was sailing upwards on top of the load. He was a brave man and he kept his head. He arrived at the top firing his pistol. This so surprised the cliff-top party that they also ran away, leaving him with both contraband and apparatus.

A colleague was less successful. He was ambushed by other smugglers above the white cliffs. They blindfolded him, bound his legs and shouted, 'Throw him over!' He was pushed over an edge and left hanging by his fingers. He dug his nails into the grass and hung on to the limit of endurance. – Then he dropped. He fell two feet into a chalk pit.

These stories fit a popular idea of smugglers – cheerful, reckless fellows, good at heart. They were not often so. Far more frequently they were cruel thugs. Towards the middle of the eighteenth century when they reached the height of their power they ganged up into bands several hundred strong. They cared for no man, customs officers and troops included. There are recorded instances of long trains of horses laden with tea being led quite openly through Kent, of six tons of tea a week being run into Sussex from France. The smugglers ruled by fear. If any were taken they were likely enough to be acquitted because magistrates and juries were afraid to convict. It made no difference whether they handled gentle tea or fiery spirits. They were in it for the money and bad luck to anyone who even looked like getting in their way. If there had been a heavy duty on Bibles they would probably have been smuggled by methods as ruthless.

The law itself was largely to blame for this. The authorities, desperately worried about the enormous loss of revenue if not about the general lack of civic discipline, imposed penalties of increasing severity. Almost every form of smuggling, even assembling for the purpose of running contraband goods, became a capital offence. Yet the Act of 1736, although it came early in the series, was the worst of the lot because it aimed to encourage the informer. A smuggler could obtain a free pardon by disclosing his offences and the names of all those with whom he had been associated.

This Act defeated its avowed purpose. Since the associates were almost certainly due to be hanged if caught in any case they did not hesitate to murder, generally after torture, anyone who even looked like being an informer. The smugglers saw to it that those killings were of the sort to be generally talked about and known. Thus even large rewards for information went unclaimed. The authorities had to depend on anonymous letters and on a few captured smugglers certain of conviction who turned King's evidence to save their skins.

A picture of smuggling as it really was is painted crude and large in *A Genuine History of the Inhuman Murders of William Galley, a Custom-House Officer of the Port of Southampton and David Chuter, Shoemaker* 'Written by a Gentleman at Chichester and published at the request of the Gentlemen of the County of Sussex; in order to prevent the world from being amus'd with false and ficticious Relations'. It was published in 1749 and gives the warning that 'Whoever shall presume to pyrate it, or any part thereof, will be prosecuted as the Law directs'. But we will have to risk that. The other main sources used here are the evidence and confessions in the subsequent trials.

But first the background. Well before the middle of the eighteenth century the day of the small-scale free trader had passed. As the racket grew so did the organizations which worked it. A large band could deal in whole shiploads of smuggled goods. Besides, there was greater safety in numbers, for the revenue men might be overawed and the whole countryside terrorized into acquiescence.

Kent and Sussex had a particularly bad reputation. They were the area covered by the Hawkhurst gang. (The word gang really was used then in ordinary unmelodramatic speech.) Their members boasted that they could muster 500 men within an hour or two. They were not content with smuggling, but between runs practised burglary and highway robbery with violence. When they wanted horses to carry their goods they commandeered them. They did exactly as they liked. An example of their sense of humour was spreadeagling two customs men on the sand at low water and leaving them to be drowned by the rising tide. The village of Goudhurst, which offended them, they threatened to burn to the ground on a given day. In their attempt to carry out this threat they were successfully resisted, losing two men dead and several prisoners. It is significant that the villagers had to depend entirely on themselves for their defence and that the news value of the incident was not considered worth more than half an inch in the *Gentleman's Magazine* of April 1747. 'Two smugglers, George Kingsman and Barnet Wollit, both outlaws, the first of which formerly killed a man on Hurst Green, were killed in a skirmish with the townsmen of Goudhurst, in Kent, who found it necessary to arm against these desperadoes, who rob and plunder, and live upon the spoil wherever they come.'

The leader of the gang was Thomas Kingsmill, 28 years old. (In spite of the difference in spelling he appears to have been a brother of the George Kingsman mentioned above.) His lieutenant was a partly crippled carpenter named Perin. Perin had a head for business and was employed in making purchases across the Channel.

In September 1747 he went to Guernsey in the cutter *The Three Brothers* and bought 37 cwt of tea for £500 – a biggish investment. The plan was to run this somewhere on the Sussex coast, but on the way back *The Three Brothers* was intercepted by a revenue cutter commanded by Captain William Johnson. Perin's boat turned downwind, north-westward, and Johnson followed with all sail set. For six hours the two craft raced. They were of similar rig and it was a close thing all the way. But at last Johnson got within range and started firing, whereupon the smugglers took to their ship's boat and rowed for it. They got clear away, which seems peculiar. But Johnson could hardly have captured both the cutter and her crew once they had abandoned ship. At any rate he was content with ship and cargo, which he brought into Poole, the tea being locked up in the Customs House.

When Perin got back with the news it caused a storm. Kingsmill was not the sort to accept defeat. A party of sixty armed men was organized to win back the tea. They met at Rowlands Castle, all of them armed and with a baggage horse carrying heavier weapons. They marched to Lyndhurst where they lay up in the forest during the day of 6 October, and set off for Poole 'in the glimpse of the evening'.

Before midnight they were on the outskirts of the town, and sent two men ahead to reconnoitre. One soon returned to say it was no good. A sloop was made fast against the quay and her guns would blow them to pieces if they approached the Customs House door.

'If you will not do it, we will do it ourselves,' Kingsmill shouted. It seems there were others besides his own men present. But he rallied them all. A more thorough examination showed that the low tide would make it impossible for the sloop to bring her guns to bear on their objective.

Leaving thirty men to guard their rear, the rest went forward to the attack. They met no resistance and found little difficulty in breaking into the Customs House. They took all the tea – except, for some reason, a bag of 5 lb – and withdrew into the New Forest. There they weighed and divided up the booty.

Next day, without any attempt at secrecy, they started home. They were riding through Fordingbridge where a large crowd had turned to watch the cavalcade go by when John Diamond, one of the smugglers, spotted a friend in the crowd. This was a shoemaker named Daniel Chater with whom he had once worked at harvest-time. He stopped to shake hands and talk to him for a minute before continuing after the others.

Although hundreds of people must have seen the cavalcade before it broke up in Sussex and Kent, nobody knew anything when the authorities started asking questions. A large reward was offered for information. None was forthcoming. Thus three months went by.

Then Diamond was arrested on suspicion. There was no evidence against him but he was held in Chichester prison. This caused gossip, and Chater the shoemaker who was evidently a silly fellow bragged to acquaintances about his meeting with the prisoner the morning after the raid. This came to the ears of the chief of Customs at Southampton who arranged that one of his subordinates, William Galley, should accompany Chater into Sussex, bearing a letter to Major Battin, Justice of the Peace at Chichester, asking him to interrogate Chater with regard to Diamond.

The two men set off on horseback, for Chichester on 14 February. On the way they called at the house of an acquaintance of Chater. The talkative shoemaker told their errand – which was, of course, no less than informing – and was himself informed that Major Battin was not at Chichester but at his house near Rowlands Castle.

Going on through Leigh, they called at the New Inn to ask the way to Rowlands Castle. Two brothers named Austin and their brother-in-law offered to guide them. Thus, about noon, they reached the White Hart at Rowlands Castle and stopped for a glass of rum.

This inn was kept by widow Payne whose five sons were smugglers. She suspected something – it could only have been by intuition – and questioned one of the Austins about the strangers. He in all innocence answered with what Chater had told him, that they were taking a letter to Major Battin, J.P.

At this widow Payne sent one of her sons for William Jackson and William Carter, while another son fetched William Steele, Samuel Downer known as Little Sam, Edmond Richards, and Henry Shearman who was called Little Harry.

All these were smugglers. They sat down to 'a pot of hot' and got into conversation with the strangers.

Something must have come out, for Jackson soon took Chater into the yard and asked him point-blank where Diamond was. 'Chater said he believed he was in custody, but how he did not know; but that he was going to appear against him, which he was sorry for, but could not help it.'

Here Galley called warningly to his companion. Jackson knocked him down with a blow in the face. Galley had already wanted to be gone, but had been put off by widow Payne saying that the boy with the stable key was away for the moment. Now he made another attempt to go. Instead of doing this, however, he and Chater were persuaded to return to the kitchen for another drink.

They were made intoxicated and put to bed in the next room. Their pockets were searched, the letter found and read aloud. While the two men slumbered the smugglers discussed what they should do with them. The first suggestions were quite mild – to take them to France or keep them concealed until the fate of Diamond was known. But the wives of some of the smugglers then appeared and demanded much more violent action. 'Hang them, for they come here to hang us!' they shouted. Galley and Chater were peacefully sleeping – until Jackson jumped on to the bed and spurred them on the forehead. Having thus wakened them he whipped them back into the kitchen.

After this they were placed upon a horse with their legs tied under its body, and were whipped along the road. They toppled sideways and hung upside down. Still mercilessly they were whipped. That he might better feel the punishment, Galley's coat was taken off and left all bloody on the road. They were kicked and slashed with knives. Galley begged them to kill him. 'No, G – d d – n your b – d,' said Jackson, 'if that's the case we must have something more to say to you.' More whipping followed and then Little Sam got up behind Galley on the horse and tortured him in a way as crude and sickening as it was simple. The Gentleman of Chichester is too much of a gentleman to write swear words in full, but he gives every detail of the treatment. There are pages of it, for the smugglers took time off to drink before going back to work. But the end, delayed as long as possible, came at last. Galley was buried alive. Chater was thrown down an empty well, and stones and logs were hurled on top of him until his groaning ceased.

The murderers then tried to dispose of the two horses. They killed Galley's, cut it up and buried it. Chater's got away and returned to its master. But, writes the Gentleman of Chichester, Mr Shearer, Chief of Southampton Customs, who had hired Galley's horse 'was obliged to pay for it'.

A runaway horse and Galley's bloody coat were the only clues, for nobody talked, of course. After seven months it looked as if nothing more would be discovered.

Then a magistrate received an anonymous letter telling where Galley was buried. He was found with his hands covering his face. Another letter led the searchers to the well where Chater's mangled body lay. Yet another letter – and William Steele was arrested. He at once turned King's evidence which helped in the rounding up of the rest. In due course they were all hanged, except Jackson who died shortly after his sentence had been pronounced.

This was very far from being the end of smuggling, for there were any number of other gangs at work. They flourished not only in the districts mentioned, but all round the coasts of the British Isles. The old story of big runs continued whatever the Government might do in its attempts to stop them.

How did it end? Large-scale smuggling of spirits, tobacco, silk and so on was not put down until after the battle of Waterloo when the country had time and troops to spare to put its house in order. But the smuggling of tea was stopped thirty-one years earlier than that by a very simple act – an act of law. In 1784 Pitt repealed the high duties and at the same time compelled the East India Company to import enough tea to satisfy demands without raising prices. Thereafter honest traders could compete with smugglers. Those in the racket were outraged. In Scotland they called it the burning and starving act.

It seems appropriate to end this chapter with a smuggler's epitaph.

> A little tea: one leaf I did not steal
> For guiltless bloodshed I to God appeal.
> Put tea in one scale, human blood in t'other,
> And think what 'tis to slay a harmless brother.

CHAPTER IV

Back in China

Tea is like the East he grows in,
A great yellow Mandarin
With urbanity of manner
And unconsciousness of sin.
                    G. K. Chesterton

ALL the tea we have been talking of was grown in China, and
Canton was still the only port open to foreign ships.

It will be remembered that the Honourable East India Company – or John Company as it came to be familiarly called – had
been granted a monopoly of Oriental trade in 1600. Though
slow to get a foot inside the Chinese door, it had during the
late seventeenth century and throughout the eighteenth con-
solidated and built up its position until it represented by far
the biggest organization of any foreign power. Indeed it was
the greatest trading monopoly there has ever been in the world.
The French, Dutch, Danes, Spaniards and Swedes had come
to Canton but gradually reduced or closed their establishments.
The Americans had come, and stayed in increasing numbers.
But the East India Company and a few English and Parsee firms
which traded under its licence formed by far the biggest unit.

John Company's monopoly was coming to an end at last.
The Company had hoped to have it renewed for China as it
had so often been before at the end of each fresh lease of life
But it had ended in India in 1813 although the Company
remained powerful there until the Mutiny. The growing army
of private traders – middle-class industrial England coming
into its own – persuaded Parliament that it should *not* be re-

newed for China after the year 1833. This caused great changes which helped to bring to a crisis the thoroughly unsatisfactory conditions of trade which had existed for so long. It is high time we went back to China.

The season to approach Canton was the three months, June to August, when the south-west monsoon was blowing. (October to April was the time to leave, for then the prevailing wind was from the opposite direction.) Let us imagine an approach in August. The wind is so light that even with all sail set – including studding sails which are the equivalent of a yacht's spinnaker – the beautiful wooden ship of about a thousand tons glides almost imperceptibly through the smooth water. It is very hot: a burning, dazzling sky above, below a glassy surface broken occasionally by the athletics of bonetas and albecores. A booby flaps lazily among the rigging. Apart from the tiny island of Pulu Sapatu there has been nothing else to see since leaving the Straits of Malacca ten days ago. It has been a four months' voyage from England and we are impatient to arrive.

A blue haze appears in front. Very gradually – for we are moving only at a strolling pace – this forms into a group of islands, the Ladrones, off the mouth of Canton Bay. The steep slopes of the more fertile islands have been shaped into terraces by generations of patient husbandmen. On those which are barren are the houses of fishermen. One of these men will act as pilot through the archipelago. The boat which comes alongside has been made familiar by Chinese prints – eyes painted on the bow, high square stern, cabin amidships, lateen sail made of mats strengthened by a fan-like ribbing of bamboo. The pilot has never seen a chart, but he knows the currents and the depths of the channels at every stage of the tide. His crew of half a dozen may all belong to the same family. In any case they look very much the same to Western eyes – the 'Chinese' face, head shaved in front, a jet-black pigtail hanging down behind. The clothing of Nanking cotton (which we call nankeen) consists of a long smock and shortish trousers from which the ankles and bare feet project. These are cheerful, simple, hardy people, always the same at heart whoever rules them.

This pilot takes us to Macao Roads. Here we must wait for a licensed pilot and the chop, the written permission to proceed.

This is the first taste of Chinese officialdom, a mixture of Confucian calm and laborious bureaucracy, so we may have to wait some time.

There is leisure to observe Macao. It has grown since Weddell's day. The Eight Regulations are still in force and the hundred-odd Europeans and Americans who work at Canton from August to March must keep their womenfolk and children here, and join them in the off-season. Now, in August, these merchants have just gone up-river, and in the heat of the afternoon the town seems dead. There is very little shipping in the harbour, for Macao was by-passed when Canton was opened. It looks like a sleepy, faded place on the coast of Portugal – the white houses clustering on the steep slope above the bay, the numerous churches, the fort whose guns have sometimes fired in salute but never in anger for a couple of centuries or more. The Iberian impression is increased when, in the cool of the evening, the Portuguese wake from their siestas and come out to stroll by the sea along the Playa Grande in formal evening dress, greeting the acquaintances they pass. Since everyone knows everybody there is a great deal of bowing.

With the chop granted, we sail on. In the first chapter brief mention was made of Lintin Island in the middle of Canton Bay. Then its name, the Solitary Nail, was appropriate. But by 1830 its waters have become crowded with shipping – beautiful, sleek, sailing craft with raked back masts; a number of unrigged but well-armed hulks evidently used for storage; long, narrow Chinese boats with fifty oars or more; a general air of activity. The uninstructed traveller might well wonder what was going on in this poor anchorage over sixty miles from the trading post. It was as if, approaching Greenock up the Clyde, one saw a host of shipping around Ailsa Craig. Of course there was a very good reason for the crowd and bustle at Lintin but although this was an open secret it was not talked about to strangers by the servants of the Honourable Company. It was, they were careful to point out, nothing to do with them.

Twenty miles after passing Lintin, with the wind still fair, one reaches the Bogue. In this narrow channel between hills the sailing may be difficult. But having paid the dues and received the chop there is no threat or opposition from the five ferocious-looking forts – which are all in fact just as impotent as they were 200 years ago.

So the ship sails on, the Chinese pilot stalking up and down the bridge with an expression of the utmost gravity, now and then giving such orders as, 'Mizzee-topsail itte sick – makee die', which the sailors have learnt to understand.

It will be remembered that beyond Tiger Island at the inland end of the Bogue the hills fall away and the great rice plain opens out. This scene is still the same – the blue-clad workers in the fields, the fishermen in the shallow, muddy creeks of the meandering deltaic river. But in the 1830s as the traveller's ship advanced he saw in front a forest of tall masts apparently growing out of the land. He was looking over the flat curving banks at the anchorage of Whampoa. The river brought him there after thirty miles of serpentine wandering.

This was as far up the Pearl River as the regulations – and the depth of water – allowed foreign ships to go. Whampoa was not much of a place, a squalid village on a muddy island, but ships had to wait there for three or four months for the tea to be brought down to Canton from the up-country growing areas and then shipped on by barge. The delay would be longer if there were trouble or if a ship had arrived early in the season to get the best of both the selling and buying markets. She could not start home before October when the north-east monsoon began to blow, for these sturdy ships could not effectively beat against the wind.

Dr Toogood Downing, who has been the main source of information for this chapter so far, describes his arrival at Whampoa, his own ship dressed with flags and the band playing.

> 'Here conjugated together and collected from different nations many thousands of miles asunder, is to be seen a fleet of between fifty to sixty sail of the finest vessels which, with the exception of those of the Navy, are ever sent upon the ocean ... The single and double sterns of the ships, painted in various styles according to the individual or national taste, disclose the names of many a well-known merchantman; while fluttering above them in the breeze and giving life and spirit to the whole are seen the national ensigns dyed with a variety of brilliant colours. The scarlet flag of Great Britain waving from some of the largest ships is seen

in juxtaposition with the yellow emblem of Spain, and the tricolour of the French and the Dutchman. That red flag with swallow tails belongs to a Dane, while the starred and streaked ensign of the vessel running up in shore distinguishes the American on his way to join his fellow-countrymen. Large cargo-boats and junks, some of them highly adorned, are seen winding their way with great skill between the Indiamen, while the whole surface of the water appears covered with an infinity of small craft, paddling about in every direction . . .

'As the ship enters Whampoa Reach to take up her position with the others in the first convenient vacant space, the anchor is got ready and the sails not in use are unbent. Slowly she proceeds, and at last, when near the place which has been chosen for her, the topsails are lowered and clewed up and the order "Let go the anchor" is pronounced.

Before this time, however, the vessel is surrounded by a host of washboats. By the time she is at her station she is dragging six or eight of these attachés along after her, one fastening and holding on to the other like a cluster of bees, and it must be a very ill-natured person indeed who would oblige them to let go their hold.'

Each of these floating laundries is crewed by three or four Chinese girls.

'Their red good-natured faces are to be seen peeping out of the matting (which covers the cabin) and always with a smile or laugh at your service. These girls are rather under the usual size, healthy, active and robust . . . A stranger finds a great deal of difficulty at first sight in distinguishing a male from a female as he passes up the river. The only characteristic is to be seen in the appearance of the head, the hair of which in the male is always shaved off in front, whilst in the female it is allowed to remain as nature designed it. Small, plain rings are placed in the ears; the face is full and oval and with only a slight, sometimes not apparent, tightness of the semilunar arch of the eyelid, and rows of regular beautiful teeth. On the whole the wash-girls may be considered good looking, some of them indeed very pretty, and together with their good-natured laughing countenance and remarkably musical voices give you a favourable impression of their sex in this country. . . .

'As it depends entirely on the option of the chief-mate to allow wash-girls to come on board to solicit employment they climb up and stand upon the gangway, or often bawl out from their boats and try to gain his goodwill by every means in their power. "Ah, you missee chiefee matee, how you dooa? I saavey you long tim, when you catchee Whampoa last tim. How missee captainee? I saavey him werry wen. You saavey my? I makee mendee, all same you shirtee last tim."'

The sailors were not allowed ashore at Whampoa, but the land came to them. There were barbers' boats, shop boats which offered food, clothes, toys, anything for sale. There were fortune-tellers' boats and theatrical company boats. It was a floating city. But before the ship's company could have any dealings with them there was much official business to be done.

The compradore was soon on board. He was a cog in the over-complicated trading machinery. He acted as middleman between ships' pursers and the Chinese caterers from whom they bought stores, it being Chinese policy to prevent the barbarians having any dealings with the common people of the land. The compradore system was tiresome and bureaucratic. But, *personally*, Olo Ackow (Olo is pidgin for old) was a friend of everyone on board. He recognized anyone who had been to Whampoa before, and they greeted him with warm hand-shakes. He stretched his duty and went out of his way to be obliging.

Next came the Grand Hoppo's junior representative, known as Jack Hoppo. A junk was made fast to each side of the ship, and an official was sent on board to ensure that nothing was smuggled ashore. But again there was a human side to it. Jack Hoppo was the best man to approach if you wanted to arrange a bit of 'smug pidgin', meaning smuggling.

The hatches, though, were still secured. They could not be opened until a second – and more impressive – batch of the Hoppo's men had visited the ship to fix and receive the harbour dues. This might not happen for some days. It was a formal affair, the mandarin in charge being piped on board and a large retinue following.

Business did not begin at once. That would have been the worst possible etiquette. First must come wine, biscuits and small talk. Then measurements were taken of the ship's length and beam and an equivalent of tonnage calculated. On this the charge was based: it was not a fixed amount. Whatever it might be it was unlikely to exceed the 'cumshaw', the official tip.

These two sums together, plus certain minor charges, secured the Hoppo's 'opening barrier fee'.

That opened the holds. The imported cargo was unloaded and sent up-river to Canton in 'chops'. (In this case this useful word means barges.) It would be three or four months before the tea was brought down-river to be loaded. The merchants who bought this and other commodities had long ceased to be supercargoes of the ships concerned. They remained in China, working in Canton or relaxing in Macao. The months during which the fleet waited for its cargoes was for these businessmen a period of intense activity. But for the sailors there was practically nothing to do except get into trouble. They managed pretty well. By long-established custom they got an occasional day in Canton.

The liberty boat was rowed by the liberty men, thirteen miles up-river, with a junior officer at the tiller. It was a hard pull in the heat, but after months of sobriety and celibacy Jack Tar would have gone ten times the distance for a few hours of shore leave. Half-way he claimed a tot of rum – this was another tradition – and for the rest of the time sweated along through an ever-growing crowd of shipping. Besides busily moving vessels large and small there were huge rafts of timber, fishing stakes with nets stretched between them, a host of houseboats. Thousands of Chinese lived permanently on the water. They were a lawless crowd who hurled insults and refuse at the foreign devils as they passed. They expressed an inborn hatred for beings different from themselves. There were more elegant craft besides – the 'flower boats' on which ladies with tiny feet whispered, giggled and made suggestive signs. But these were for the Chinese only. A European who boarded one was never seen again.

As the crowd of shipping increased so did the noise. There was an incessant clamour of gongs, the crackle of fireworks, the cackle of voices. During the final phase of the journey this last was deafening, for to reach the landing stage of the Factories the ship's boat had to force a way down a narrow lane of anchored vessels already crowded with moving traffic, using oars as punt poles. Each collision set off explosions of abuse.

The city of Canton was contained by a quadrangle of high

A family at tea. From an oil painting by an unknown English artist, *circa* 1725, in the Victoria and Albert Museum

The East Indiaman *Earl of Balcarris,* 1,417 tons, off the China coast. From an oil painting by W. J. Huggins, 1824

A clipper by an unknown Chinese artist

walls, each side more than a mile in length. The port, a straggle of suburbs and the factories were outside the walls. The factories consisted of warehouses, offices and living quarters. They were of two or three storeys, built in a row against each other, except where a couple of narrow streets, Old China Street and Hog Lane, cut through the blocks. The factories still occupied by their nationals flew their flags on poles before their doors. A small square separated the buildings from the wharves and water steps, and in front of the British factory was a walled garden.

W. C. Hunter, an American businessman who was in China during the period under review, gives an impression of the style maintained by the East India Company.

'Soon after I landed in Canton I had the honour of a first invitation to dine with the Factory, and must confess that at my age I accepted it with fear and trepidation. One of the *invité* from the Suy-Hong, Mr Oliver H. Gordon, accompanied me. Our way led through the great outer gate, past the chapel whose spire bore conspicuously a large clock, the only one in Canton, and by which everyone regulated his watch; then up a broad flight of stone steps to a verandah, crossing which one entered the library and reception-room as well. When the hosts and the guests had assembled, large folding doors were opened and we entered the noble dining-room whose brilliancy and cheerfulness and gorgeously furnished table I see *now*. At the remote end of the room were grouped the Chinese servants of the Factory and of the guests, in caps and long robes, who immediately took up their places behind their respective masters as soon as seated.'

The Chinese called the British factory 'Assured Tranquillity'; the American, 'Wide Fountains'.

The Chinese expressed a like fancy in the legends above their doors in Hog Lane and Old China Street – 'May wealth flow in abundantly', 'Rich customers are perpetually welcome'; on their furniture or the goods they offered – 'The bucket of superlative peace', 'The box of great tranquillity'; and still more in their shop names – 'Peace and quiet', 'Current gains', 'Collective justice'. The common sailors had to find their amusement in these streets which sometimes belied their pacific inscriptions. In the numerous drinking dens the brew offered was a mixture of alcohol, tobacco juice, sugar and arsenic. Jack was soon either boisterously drunk or down and out and robbed. Hog Lane was notorious.

The sailors could exercise themselves – if they wanted to – in the square in front of the factories. But in fact it was generally crowded with Chinese hawkers and loiterers trying to sell things to the barbarians or merely staring at them.

Once a ship's band in uniform was brought up-river to entertain the men on shore leave. The Chinese gaped. One of them asked, 'What for he makee so muchee noisee?'

'Noise!' answered a barbarian. 'May Foo (Buddha) run away with you. That no belong noise, belong music. You no likee?'

'Hai-yah,' the Chinaman exclaimed. 'My how can likee? All makee mixee. *My* China music number one. *He* too muchee foolo —'

He broke off and ran away with a hand to his behind, shouting over his shoulder, 'What for you kick my?'

Fights were common, but serious trouble very rare indeed. The mandarins, as all officials were called, saw to it that the foreign devils were as safe in Canton as in their own home towns.

II

Safe, but as tiresomely restricted as they had been when they first came to Canton a century and a half before. In the last section we saw something of the unofficial relationship between the foreigners and the lower orders of the Chinese. Now we will examine the official or business side.

The Europeans and Americans still only had contact with the Hong merchants. They could do business with no one else, anywhere else in China. The Cantonese would take few Western goods. The British could offer nothing that they really wanted. So Britain had to buy with silver the tea which she wanted in greater quantities every year.

This was a maddening situation. The Western traders were on excellent terms with the Hong merchants. Like Olo Ackow, the compradore, they were in their official capacity a nuisance, an obstruction, but they were personally charming. Worst of all, although it was obligatory to trade with them they had no power to alter the conditions of trade even in the smallest degree.

The ruler of the province of Canton was the Viceroy, the Celestial Emperor's personal representative. He was far out of reach, completely unapproachable. But the Hoppo was in charge of trade. He could have smoothed out difficulties if he had wanted to. But he remained almost as aloof as the Viceroy, considering it far below his dignity to have any personal contact with barbarians.

It so happened that soon after Dr Dowding's arrival in Canton a new Grand Hoppo was appointed. Dowding's first-hand account of a visit paid by this dignitary to the English factory is of considerable interest as demonstrating the attitude of the higher officials.

'I happened to be in Canton on the day when the new Hoppo was installed into his office, and had thus an opportunity of seeing the great man when he came into the suburbs. On this occasion, and on no other as I was informed, does he show himself to the foreigners, but keeps himself retired within the city walls. The cause of his honouring the Fan-quis with this visit, was doubtless in order that he might know something of the people over whom he was going to exercise his authority. Upon my asking a native, however, for the reason, he told me that the Hoppo would shortly have an audience of the emperor, when his majesty would probably ask him what kind of people the Fan-quis were, and he should look very foolish, if he were to answer that he had not seen them. He therefore paid them this visit, that he might be able to give a better account of them than many of his predecessors, who had never seen the Fan-quis at all.

'Due notice was sent to the resident merchants some time before the intended visit, in order that they might be properly prepared to receive the Tartar grandee; and, on the morning in question, the procession moved swiftly through the principal streets of the suburbs.

'The Hoppo sat in his state carriage, borne along by many coolies, accompanied by the Hong merchants in their sedans, and preceded by the usual number of officers to clear the way. They were received in the state-rooms of The British Factory, and after the preliminary ceremonies had been performed on both sides, the Hoppo was invited by the Fan-quis to partake of a breakfast which had been provided for the occasion.

'A great number of foreigners had collected outside the

building, anxious to get a sight of the man in office. As they were admitted into the house, I, among the rest, had an opportunity of satisfying my curiosity. Within the principal entrances were all the carriages placed upon the pavement, with the coolies loitering about, or reclining on the ground taking their rest. Beyond them, in the great hall on the ground floor, were the Hong merchants, seated in armchairs placed in a row against the wall. Their countenances were grave and dignified, and they possessed the grand requisite of manly beauty in China, every one of them being of portly dimensions. Their clothes were formed of the brightest-coloured silks, and were rich in embroidery.

'Casting but a hasty glance at these silent security-men, we ascended the stairs, and after passing along a corridor partially filled with loitering waiters, we entered the state-rooms, and took up our station with the rest of the foreigners.

'Along the centre of the spacious apartment a table was placed, spread with a snow-white cloth, and covered with dishes of the greatest delicacies in season. Blanc-manges, jellies, and fruits, were abundantly supplied, in addition to the more substantial viands; and, in fact, everything necessary to form a first-rate breakfast after the English fashion.

'On a handsome chair somewhat resembling a throne, placed at the head of this tempting board, sat the Hoppo, surrounded by his numerous attendants respectfully attending to his wishes. He was an old man of about sixty years of age, and of rather a prepossessing countenance. A few grey hairs were growing from the upper lip, and a small tuft of beard was depending from his chin. Attached to the handsome mandarin cap which he wore, a portion of the tail feather of a peacock was to be seen when he turned his head on one side. This honorary badge had been given him by his sovereign as a mark of personal favour, and together with the ruby globe which surmounted the cap, indicated the high rank which he filled in the state.

'As this was a day of ceremony, the old gentleman had got on his best apparel, or more properly speaking, he wore his court-dress. The materials were of the finest quality, the colours chiefly blue and red, and richly embroidered. Around his neck hung a row of large beads, depending below the waist, while on the breast was to be seen the silken badge, whereon the figure of a bird was curiously represented in needlework.

'The attendants on the grandee consisted of his secretary, his linguist, and many of his friends, who were dressed in an equally gay style, but did not show so noble a button on the tops of their hats. Some of the natives in waiting were uncovered, and were clothed in the plain habits of menials.

'In order that the Hoppo might have a good view of the Fan-quis, and vice versa, a slight bannister was fastened up at a little distance on one side of the table. Behind this barrier all the foreigners stood, facing the Chinaman, and watching every movement of his goodnatured countenance.

'The old man eyed the good things upon the table, and, as he had the whole of them to himself, no one presuming to take a seat, he whispered to his attendants to fetch them for him. As each dish was brought successively, and held up to his eye, he examined it very carefully all around as an object of great curiosity, and then languishingly shook his head, as a sign for it to be taken away. Thus he proceeded for a considerable time, until he had looked at everything on the table, without finding a single article suitable to his delicate stomach.

'The foreigners all this while were looking on with very different feelings. Their appetites were wonderfully sharpened by viewing so many good things, especially as it was now the usual time for luncheon. Many of them were witty in their abuse of the old gentleman for his want of taste; and some called him an old fool, and were sorry that they were so situated that they could not show him *how to eat*. However, the Hoppo understood none of these sayings, but quietly proceeded with his examination of the exotic dainties, and when the table had been entirely ransacked, he shook his head once more in sign of disapproval, and then called for a *cup of tea*.'

He drank this slowly, oblivious of the exasperation of his hosts, then rose and left, his retinue following him.

Men of this character and outlook were not likely to bother themselves – so long as they received their dues – with the troubles of the foreign community.

So what was the state of trade? It will be interesting to look at the books of the American and British companies for 1831 which Maurice Collis analysed in his *Foreign Mud*.

In round numbers the American figures were as follows:

Imported to China		*Exported from China*	
Western goods:	2 m. dollars	Tea, etc.:	6 m. dollars
Silver:	4 m. dollars		
	6 m. dollars		

In other words they had an adverse balance of 4,000,000 dollars which was paid off with silver coin.

Now the East India Company:

Imported to China	*Exported from China*	
Western goods: 2½ m. dollars	Tea:	8 m. dollars
	Silver:	1 m. dollars
		9 m. dollars

Their adverse trade balance would appear to be 5,500,000 dollars, yet they brought back from China 1,000,000 dollars' worth of silver.

We begin to get at the explanation when we look at the figures for what were called the country firms. These were British and Parsee firms with offices in India who traded Indian goods with China by arrangement with the East India Company.

Imported to China		*Exported from China*	
Cottons:	4 m. dollars	Various goods:	5 m. dollars
Spices, etc.:	2 m. dollars	Silver:	12 m. dollars
Opium:	11 m. dollars		
	17 m. dollars		17 m. dollars

The country firms had a favourable balance of 12,000,000 dollars. They were glad to let the East India Company use as much of this silver as they wanted against bills on London, which saved them (before the days of banks) from the dangerous necessity of transporting bullion. Thus the East India Company could buy all the tea it wanted without bothering about its balance of trade.

The secret of the success of the country firms, and therefore of the East India Company, was opium. That was the commodity which the Chinese wanted – wanted so badly that they paid 11,000,000 dollars for it in one year, cash in advance.

The East India Company held a monopoly of Indian grown opium. (Turkey was the only other considerable producer of the drug.) The Company sold the crop yearly at auctions in Calcutta. There, as they were careful to point out, their responsibility ended. The opium was bought by the country firms, who re-sold it to the Chinese. That is not quite the whole story. The import of opium into China was forbidden under the severest penalties. So it was not brought to Whampoa. It was carried by small, fast ships to Lintin, the island in the middle of Canton Bay, and stored on the hulks which we mentioned as lying at anchor round that island. From there it was collected by many-oared Chinese galleys – called centipedes or scrambling dragons – and run into the innumerable creeks around the estuary. Besides being illegal it paid no duty, thus defrauding the Emperor of his due. An alternative method of disposing of the opium was for British or American vessels to carry it north along the coast and sell it there. Thus yet another regulation was broken, that of trading in ports other than Canton.

You may well ask how smuggling on this scale could be operated from a base in Canton Bay. W. C. Hunter gives an answer.

'So perfect a system of bribery existed (with which foreigners had nothing whatever to do) that the business was carried on with ease and regularity. Temporary interruptions occurred, as for instance on the installation of newly arrived magistrates. Then the question of fees arose; but was soon settled unless the newcomer was exorbitant in his demands or, as the broker would express it, "too muchee foolo". In good time, however, it would be arranged satisfactorily, the brokers re-appeared with beaming faces, and peace and immunity reigned in the land. . . .

'The Canton officials rarely made any reference to the Lintin station; but sometimes, compelled by force to do so, would issue a proclamation ordering vessels "loitering at the outer anchorage" either to come into port or sail away to their own countries lest the "dragons of war" should be opened, and with fiery discharges annihilate all who opposed this, a "special edict".'

Occasionally there were fiery discharges, but these were no more dangerous than the crackers let off to placate the spirits of wind and water. When an opium ship, having finished her business at Lintin, set sail for India, the mandarin junks cast loose their moorings and in full view of everyone ashore set out in hot pursuit. Skippers with a mischievous sense of humour might then slow down, in which case the junks had to shorten sail as well, for the last thing they really wanted to do was to come up with the enemy. But if all went well they followed the foreign ship out of sight – though not out of hearing – of the land and then started a furious bombardment. In due course a report was received in Peking of a foreign smuggler sunk or driven off.

The opium traffic provides an example of how the Chinese had perfected the art of self-deception since their once great empire had entered its second childhood, and of how corrupt their complex bureaucracy had become. Every official was in the racket, from the meanest mandarin to the Viceroy himself, and every foreign devil except a very few who had moral scruples about it. Hunter goes on, speaking for the foreigner who dealt in opium with the scrupulously honest – even if criminal – Chinese brokers: 'His sales were pleasantness and his remittances were peace. Transactions seemed to partake of the nature of the drug; they imparted a soothing frame of mind with three per cent commission on sales, one per cent on returns, and no bad debts. To the agent each chest was worth £20 sterling, one year with another.' Tens of thousands of chests passed through their hands every season.

Since this is a book about tea we cannot go into the fascinating details of opium smuggling, nor the moral question which it raises. It was not only a British trade. 'We were all equally implicated,' Hunter says. (The Americans smuggled Turkish opium.) But the point here is this: of the tea being drunk in the West – at Methodist and anti-slavery meetings, in fine drawing-rooms and poor cottages – nearly all of it was in effect bought with opium. Our hero is in bad company again.

III

The Chinese acted on the principle, in which even their more intelligent officials appear to have believed, that their Emperor was the omnipotent ruler of the whole world. Therefore the foreign merchants, although barbarians from beyond the pale of civilization, belonged to vassal races. As such they were not entitled to diplomatic representation. They were merely tradesmen who must use the tradesmen's door. But it was convenient to have one person or committee to whom orders could be issued.

While the East India Company was in Canton its Select Committee spoke for all the merchants. Being by far the largest concern it was the leader. The Company accepted the crippling, often humiliating trading conditions with apparent submission because in spite of them it had made a lot of money, having found a means of obtaining the silver necessary for buying tea.

The Company was due to leave China in April 1834, when its monopoly would end. No firm remaining in Canton was of the stature to succeed it automatically. But clearly there would have to be a leader. Viceroy Lu suggested the nomination of a leading merchant, who would of course be of the same status as the Hong. The British Cabinet, without consulting those upon the spot, created a Chief Superintendency of Trade in Canton, a post of consular status.

Whether Lord Palmerston acted from subtlety or ignorance of the conditions cannot be known. But *if* the Viceroy accepted a Chief Superintendent, the British merchants would have achieved what they had been trying to get for a century and a half – access to somebody who could do something about their troubles. It was a large if.

The man chosen by Palmerston for this delicate assignment was Lord William Napier of Meristoun, a tall, straightforward, sandy-haired Scotsman of forty-eight whose background was the Royal Navy and a sheep farming estate. With his wife and two daughters he landed at Macao in July 1834. His arrival was reported to Viceroy Lu in Canton, the Chinese patrols having quickly realized that he was a 'Barbarian Eye', an official.

Lu sent written orders to Howqua, the chief Hong merchant that Napier should be informed that, not being a merchant, he must petition through the Hong for permission to visit Canton. His petition would be forwarded by the Hong to the Viceroy, who would forward it to Peking, 'and all must respectfully wait until His Majesty deigns to send a Mandate. Then orders will be issued requiring obedience. Oppose not! A special order.'

The last thing Howqua, Mowqua, the second in seniority, and the rest of the Hong thought of doing was to oppose this order. But, as usual, they were being made responsible for the obedience of a barbarian over whom they had no control. They hurried off to Macao to stop Napier. He had already left. He reached Canton on 25 July. There Howqua and Mowqua caught up with him. He would not let them speak. He was instituting a new arrangement, he said, and would only deal with the Viceroy. He sent a letter to the Viceroy. It was returned unopened. Lu would not accept any communication other than a 'petition' sent through the Hong.

At the same time he told the Hong that unless they got rid of Napier at once they would be severely punished. 'Say not that you have not been forewarned. Tremble hereat. Intensely tremble.'

Howqua and Mowqua trembled, but they could not persuade Napier to go, even when they tactfully suggested that Macao would be more healthy for him. The noble lord's temper was not improved by discovering that in the Viceroy's communications he was referred to as 'Laboriously Vile'. He refused to accept the Viceroy's orders.

Thus a hot July came to an end, the two principals not knowing – at least officially – what each had written to the other. Napier felt that sooner or later the Viceroy would be bound to accept his letter so that he could report its contents to Peking, and by accepting it he would thereby accept the principle that the Superintendent of Trade had the right to go above the heads of the Hong – and even the Hoppo – to knock at the front door, in fact.

Instead, Lu gave orders for the partial closure of trade.

Napier's riposte was scarcely diplomatic. Believing that the Chinese public was in favour of freer trade, he caused notices to be put up outside the town describing the obstructive actions of their rulers.

Lu replied with a much more forthright notice setting out his side of the affair. He made the stoppage of trade complete. He went further. He threw a cordon of troops round the British factory and on pain of death ordered all their Chinese servants to leave them, and shopkeepers to refuse them supplies.

Napier was furious. From this distance in time one may

smile, but he deserves sympathy. As a midshipman he had assisted in the great victory of Trafalgar. He had seen Napoleon defeated, seen his country rise to unquestioned leadership of the world – unquestioned in the West. In middle age he had been nominated to settle certain minor problems with an anachronistic Eastern state. To his shocked surprise they treated him as some sort of adventurer of a petty, primitive tribe who must *petition* through the usual channels even for leave to remain within the realm of the world's only civilization. He did not see the joke, as did the merchants, of being called a barbarian. He was not a personal friend of Howqua and Mowqua, who smiled and bowed, their delicate hands hidden in their wide sleeves, and most urbanely conducted themselves in an impossible situation. He was a logical Scot. Also, the Hong merchants had unwittingly been right. The sea airs of Macao would have been much more healthy. The damp heat of Canton brought on a fever. When a cool head was most necessary Napier had a high temperature. Being forced – he, the crown-appointed representative of the greatest country in the world – to make his own bed and boil his own egg (almost literally) and sue for favour like a vagabond tinker, he would show these primitives where power lay!

The only power at his immediate command was the frigate he had arrived in and another which had joined her. They were below the Bogue. Napier ordered them up to Whampoa.

They had the wind against them, and all five forts opposed their passage. But they fought their way through almost without damage. When they reached Whampoa Napier sent a threatening letter to the Viceroy. Lu did not bother to reply to it. Instead he blocked the river above and below the frigates and prepared fire-boats to send against them. 'Laboriously Vile' had played into his hands by giving him two valuable hostages.

Napier, a very sick man by this time, had to realize that for all Britain's might he and the merchants were helpless in Canton. He was carried down – through Chinese clemency – to Macao, where he died. Thus ignominiously ended an attempt to force the Emperor's hand.

There followed a period of quiescence. Napier's successors – first Sir Francis Davies and then Sir George Robinson –

lacked both clear instructions and firm backing by the distant British government, so they remained in Macao and did nothing. In December 1836 Captain Charles Elliot, R.N., inherited the unenviable post. By petitioning humbly through the proper channels he was permitted to go to Canton. But the Chinese authorities consequently treated him as no more than a chief merchant, so he had no power to negotiate for a freer trade. The British Government left him with the equivocal instructions they had given to Napier – to act as an unrecognized consul. The British merchants – since the departure of the East India Company their number had grown to over 200 – frankly despised him. They rubbed along very well with the Hong members, dining and chaffing with them. They treated the Chinese authorities as a joke, laughing at their periodic threats about opium smuggling, which was understandable since the Viceroy was one of their best customers. Elliot strongly disapproved of this traffic yet had no power to stop it. In fact he had an assignment which he discharged with the lack of aplomb which it deserved.

More and more we are becoming concerned with opium smuggling because the increasing trade in tea increasingly depended on it. Everybody knew that a major crisis would sooner or later arise. But the British did not worry because they despised the strength of China, while on their side the Chinese believed themselves invincible.

The explosion was finally sparked off by the appointment of an honest Chinese official and the death of a coolie in a drunken brawl.

On 31 December 1838 Lin was appointed Commissioner above the heads of the Viceroy and Governor. Immediately after his arrival, two months later, he demanded the surrender of all opium held by the foreign merchants in Lintin or elsewhere. At first this order was ignored like all the rest. But Lin showed his determination by completely stopping the legitimate trade, blockading the factories more effectively than had ever been done before, putting the unfortunate Hong merchants in chains and threatening the use of armed forces.

Elliot, who as we have seen disapproved of the drug smuggling, persuaded the merchants to yield up 20,000 chests of opium, undertaking that the British Government would indemnify her nationals for their loss – which suited them very well. Elliot did this entirely on his own authority. Thus, besides saddling the Government with a bill for £2,000,000, he in its name accepted responsibility for the opium traffic which until this time had always been unacknowledged and unofficial.

When Lin had received and destroyed the opium he graciously permitted the legitimate trade to be reopened. But Elliot had had enough of being responsible for 200 British lives. He ordered the merchants down to join their families at Macao. They went, leaving the Americans to continue the tea trade for them as agents.

Lin soon realized that his triumph was not complete. He had destroyed one season's opium crop – with the result that the next was worth twice as much. The smuggling was soon worse than ever, and the British were outside his grasp.

He seized on an unfortunate incident to bring them to heel. Some British and American sailors at Hong Kong had got into a scuffle with the natives and one Chinese villager had been killed. Lin demanded the surrender of the culprit. Elliot convened a British court which failed to discover who had struck the fatal blow. He reported so to Lin, who still insisted that a scapegoat should be handed over. When this was refused he descended with a body of troops upon Macao.

This was in July 1839. Elliot was still without either reinforcements or clear instructions from Britain. He ordered all his nationals – men, women and children – on board the tea fleet which had just arrived off Hong Kong.

Had Lin and Elliot been empowered to negotiate, a tragedy might yet have been averted. But Elliot was obstinate in what he conceived to be his duty – to protect the men and women in his charge – while Lin, the fanatic, pressed on in his attempts to break down the resistance of the foreign devils. He ordered that the ships should be denied provisions.

The basic cause of the trouble was the disreputable, if necessary, trade in opium. But the first shots of the war were fired on 5 September 1839 in Elliot's determination to get food and water for the refugees.

It was a war more futile than most. When they at last arrived, the bayonets of a few thousand British troops soon pricked the bubble of Chinese omnipotence. The tea shipments were not interrupted even while the state of hostilities continued. When the war ended China was opened to the West under ordinary conditions of commerce. But no one was really better off. The indemnities were paid by China largely out of the Consoo Fund, so the British only got some of their own money back. The drug traffic continued until 1908. And although free trade and the clipper races were for a short time to invest tea from China with a fine glamour that commerce was already undermined and doomed to fade into insignificance.

CHAPTER V

The Indian Venture, and Others

> Having determined, if possible, to procure
> plants and seeds from this celebrated country
> there were but two ways of proceding in the
> business. Either Chinese agents must be em-
> ployed to go into the country and procure
> them and bring them down, or I must go
> myself.
>
> *Robert Fortune*

'AT no very distant period and from some apparently accidental
event, not only the British Nation but other foreigners might
be prohibited entering the Chinese territories. . . . Some better
guarantee should be provided for the supply of this Article
than that already furnished by the toleration of the Chinese
Government.'

The article referred to is tea, and the quotation from a
memorandum submitted by a junior official of the East India
Company. It is undated but was almost certainly written in the
early 1830s when the storm clouds were already gathering over
Canton, and the end of the East India Company's monopoly
in China was in sight. The proposal was that the Company
should 'resolutely undertake' the cultivation of tea in Nepal or
in any other place which might be congenial to it.

The memorandum lay unheeded until by fortunate chance it
came into the hands of the Governor General, Lord William
Cavendish Bentinck, who paid the idea the compliment of
adopting it as his own.

On 24 January 1834 he made this speech:

'It is not necessary that I should trouble the Council with many remarks to support the abstract question of the great advantages that India would derive from the successful introduction of the tea-plant; and the only points for consideration are whether there are no reasonable grounds for the conclusion that there must be in all the varieties of climate and soil, between the Himalayas and Cape Comorin, combinations of both that must be congenial to this particular plant, and knowledge and skill for its cultivation and for the subsequent process of preparing the leaves for use. . . . As a practical agriculturist, one inclines to think that few of the foreign herbs and plants, which are become not only naturalized but also the mainstay of our Agriculture, afforded in the first instance a greater promise of successful experiment.'

In this sanguine and energetic mood his Lordship appointed a Tea Committee. Its constitution is of considerable interest. Prior to 1833 British subjects were forbidden to live or work in India except in association with the East India Company. Lord Bentinck's choice was, therefore, limited almost exclusively to men of purely administrative experience. The only scientist was Dr Nathaniel Wallich, the Director of the Government's Botanical Gardens at Calcutta.

He was a Danish Jew, born Nathan Wolff in 1787. At the age of nineteen he had arrived in Bengal as surgeon for the Danish East India Company. This suggests self-assurance if nothing else. Forty-seven years later he was in the British Agricultural and Horticultural Society's list of members as Dr N. Wallich Esq. M.D., F.R.S., F.L.S. What lay between the boy claiming to be a surgeon and the established man of science? Unfortunately we know very little about him except as a member of the Tea Committee.

As early as 1778, before Nathan Wolff was born, the finding of indigenous tea within the bounds of India had been recorded by Sir Joseph Banks, the greatest botanist of his day. More recently a tea-tree ten feet high had been reported as growing in a garden in Katmandu (Nepal was then part of India). And only a few years before Lord Bentinck's speech specimens found in Assam had been sent to Dr Wallich for identification. He had said they were not tea but a form of camellia.

He was right to the extent that tea is a form of camellia

(*C. sinensis*, while the garden camellia is *C. japonica*)[1]. His firmly negative attitude, his refusal to inquire into Banks's report or to accept as genuine the specimens sent to his Botanic Gardens, meant that the Tea Committee started their work from scratch. Their secretary, G. J. Gordon, was dispatched to China to buy seeds and recruit labourers while, with Wallich assuming the duties of secretary, a questionnaire was sent to officials throughout India. This did not ask whether anyone had seen a tea-plant. Its object was to discover places with a particular combination of topography and climate – briefly, with a temperature varying between 30° F. and 80° F., with snow as well as frost during two months of winter, and with an altitude of not less than 3,000 feet. These, the doctor was convinced, were the conditions prevailing in the good tea districts of China. His immediate object was to find exactly similar conditions in India so that the seeds or seedlings collected by the secretary, Gordon, should be sent to those places for planting.

The questionnaire produced one most dramatic answer from Assam. Not a record of the believed ideal conditions – far from that – but actual plants, actual seeds, and 'manufactured' leaves. Wallich had turned down the earlier specimens from Assam (these had been branches only) because they came from a place with a very different climate and topography from what he believed tea required. Therefore they were not tea. For the same reason he had disparaged the extensive experiments being conducted by the Dutch in Java. But here were plants which looked exactly like tea-plants, fruits which were the same as its fruits, and processed leaves which tasted exactly like tea. Even Dr Wallich could not avoid the obvious conclusion.

The Committee reported:

'It is with feelings of the greatest possible satisfaction that we

[1] This is the Linnean nomenclature. Tea has by different botanists been called by the following variety of names: *Thea sinensis, Thea olearia, Thea chinensis, Thea sinensis, Camellia thea* and *Camellia oleosa*. Those are the names of *C. sinensis* var. *sinensis* f. *parvifolia*. There are besides *C. sinensis* var. *sinensis* f. *macrophylla* and *C. sinensis* var. *assamatica* and *C. irrawadiensis*, with a number of alternative names for each. Any practical gardener would know at a glance the difference between a camellia and a tea-plant, but one can understand that it must be much more difficult for a botanist.

are enabled to announce to His Lordship in Council, that the Tea Shrub is, beyond all doubt, indigenous in Upper Assam, being found there through an extent of country of one month's march within the Honourable Company's Territories. . . . We have no hesitation in declaring this discovery . . . to be far the most important and valuable that has ever been made on matters connected with the agricultural or commercial resources of the empire. We are perfectly confident that the tea-plant which has been brought to light will be found capable, under proper management, of being cultivated with complete success for commercial purposes, and that consequently the object of our labour may be before long fully realized.'

The prospect of being able to produce with such unexpected ease the drink which does not inebriate had gone to their heads. They recalled Gordon from China, and a scientific commission consisting of Dr Wallich, another botanist who was an Assistant Surgeon named Griffiths, and a geologist, Assistant Surgeon McClelland, set off for Upper Assam to find the most suitable places in that unsuitable land.

Wallich's original convictions apart, Assam was not the country anyone would have chosen for growing anything if it could be avoided – a jungle land with a great river as the only road. The valley of Assam is over 400 miles long and about fifty miles wide. Down this flows the Brahmaputra, a river between five and twenty miles in width – nearly as wide as the Straits of Dover – in flood an all-powerful monster which shifts its course continually, uprooting the great forest trees, sweeping whole villages away. Assam was thought of, by those who thought of it at all, as a buffer state protecting India from invasion from the north-east.

Its history is this. The Ahams, a race from the North Shan states of Upper Burma, conquered the country in the thirteenth century and ruled it for about 600 years, except for a brief interruption by the Moguls. They were still more or less in power at the time under review. There had been an almost continuous series of wars between them and neighbouring Muslims, varied by raids by the hill tribes – Nagas, Mishnis, Miris, Arbors, Daflos. By the time the British came on the scene the state of the country was deplorable. They were tempted to let the contending factions fight it out on their own. But their war with

68

Burma took them into the country. When Colonel Richards in 1824 was trying to drive the Burmese out of Assam he was temporarily forced to withdraw through lack of supplies. The Burmese then skinned alive or burnt the natives who they thought had aided him. The people scattered into the jungle where very many died, leaving their cultivated land to go to waste. That does not take long in the jungle.

You find Scotsmen everywhere. In those troubled times there was one in Assam, a Robert Bruce, later Major of the Bengal Artillery and at that time trading on his own. He seems to have been a non-hero of romance who mixed himself up quite fearlessly in all the factions which were going, entirely for his own advantage. He fought with one party, was captured, changed sides, fought again – possibly made money, certainly lived as suited him. One would like to follow him further. But his significance in this story is limited if important. This rough, tough adventurer made friends with a Singhpo chief in 1823 and – eleven years before the Tea Committee was constituted – learned about the production of tea from indigenous plants by these primitive tribes.

Robert Bruce was not the sort to have a written record. But before he died, which must have been soon after this, he told his brother Charles about it. Charles Bruce was in command of a flotilla of gun-boats – meaning any sort of craft with a gun fixed forrard which could ride those waters. He followed up his brother's tip, penetrated to the district where the natives made tea from the wild growing plants, collected specimens and gave them to David Scott. Scott was one of those administrators who don't just follow in the wake of wars, but move with them, pacifying, advising and helping to reconstruct. He died on the job at forty-five and was, I believe, a splendid man. He forwarded the specimens to the Botanic Gardens in Calcutta – to be turned down by Dr Wallich eight years before the Tea Committee was formed.

To return to the Tea Committee. This questionnaire went to all District Commissioners, including Francis Jenkins who was responsible for a large area in Assam. He sent it on to his subordinates. One of these was Charles Bruce who eventually told the story of how he had followed up the information given to his brother Robert by the Singhpo chief and collected the specimens already referred to. Another subordinate, Lieutenant Andrew Charlton, sent the specimens with this letter:

> 'I have now the pleasure of sending you some seeds and leaves of tea-trees of Assam, and am sorry that the unsettled state I have been in for the last three months has prevented me sending them as soon as I intended. The leaves you could have had before but I was anxious to make them into something like tea, the best test that the tree is not a camellia as Dr Wallich imagines. . . .'

That Gordon was recalled on receipt of those specimens suggests that the Committee, in their first enthusiasm, believed that the indigenous tea would do; but they evidently had second thoughts about this very soon, for Gordon was at once sent off again. The age-old belief persisted that China was the only source of good tea. In any case the possession of seeds and plants was only the first step in founding an industry. There was the mystery of how the plants should be brought to the ideal state for harvesting, and then how the green leaves could be transformed into the marketable article.

For 150 years Western merchants had been buying tea in Canton. But their contacts had only been with merchants like themselves. The *raison d'être* of the Hong system was to insulate foreign devils from the life of China. The Chinese merchants knew little about *how* tea was produced, and what they knew they would not tell. No Chinese would willingly give away the almost sacred secret, if only from fear. So it was very difficult to obtain the necessary knowledge.

The only book on the subject was Lu Yu's *Ch'a Ching*. In what other subject can one imagine a text-book over 1,000 years old proving of practical value? But the *Ch'a Ching* was useful to the British cultivators as it had already been to the Japanese and Dutch.

Tea had reached Japan together with Buddhism and Chinese art towards the end of the sixth century A.D. The monks fostered it and it flourished. But 200 years of civil war destroyed the gardens and almost wiped the memory from men's minds. General tea-drinking did not begin again until the thirteenth century. But after that it steadily increased, becoming popular, not only a habit of priests.

The Portuguese, the first Westerners to penetrate the Orient, never thought of growing tea themselves. The Dutch did. As early as 1684 an attempt was made to cultivate Japanese plants in Java. Nothing came of this, nor of subsequent projects – largely owing to the negative attitude of the Dutch East Indian Government – until Dr Franz van Sirdold successfully grew Japanese plants in the Botanical Gardens of Buitenzorg in 1827. This venture was encouraged by the new Commissioner General who opened experimental gardens elsewhere.

At this stage there entered on the scene a go-ahead, self-confident young man named Jacobus Isidorus Lodewijk Levjen Jacobson. He was the son of a tea-broker of Rotterdam, an expert tea-taster himself. He landed in Java on his way from Holland to Canton to sample tea for the Netherlands Trading Company. Commissioner General du Bus de Gisignies was impressed by Jacobson and pressed him into service to collect implements and workmen from China.

For the next six years – 1827 to 1833 – Jacobson acted as a sort of Scarlet Pimpernel, smuggling tea and tea men out of China, often at the risk of his life. On his first journey he collected only information. On his second he brought back eleven plants. His third was unsuccessful. But on his fourth he collected 243 plants and 150 seeds. His fifth journey was more successful still. It yielded 300,000 seeds and twelve Chinese workmen.

The workmen were the real prize. But before they could be used they were all murdered in a coolie brawl – a strange enough happening.

Jacobson went again to China. He collected 7,000,000 seeds and fifteen workmen skilled in all aspects of tea production. Serious trouble started when he attempted to get them out of the country, for the Chinese Government had put a price on his head. His vessel was chased by the mandarins. They caught his interpreter, Acheong, who was later ransomed. But Jacobson got clear away with his precious cargo and received a hero's welcome in Java.

With this material he worked for fifteen years. But in spite of his tremendous efforts the Java tea industry was not yet to flourish. It was as if there were a curse on the Chinese plants collected with such difficulty and danger. They sickened in exile, yearly losing value. China's most venerated plant has never brought profit to those who took it from its native land. Not until seeds were imported from Assam did tea succeed in Java.

II

Let us return to Assam. The Tea Committee may have suffered from a paucity of scientific knowledge, but the scientific deputation suffered even more from the propensity of scientists to be individualistic and quarrelsome. Griffiths, botanist number two, soon had not a good word to say of Dr Wallich – and he had a lot to say. Of McClelland he approved. 'I cannot conclude this part of my report,' wrote Griffiths, 'without adverting to the extremely desultory manner in which the question of tea cultivation in India has been treated by every other author who has written on the subject with the exception of Mr McClelland.'

The geologist did not believe that tea was essentially a hill plant. Wallich did. Wallich had gone so far as to admit that 'the lowest class' of tea could grow at low altitudes but he stuck to his conviction that the finest must grow high, and it is only fair to state that his ruling, however he arrived at it, was ultimately proved true in Darjeeling. Griffiths, who travelled separately and, it would appear, got a little out of touch with what was happening, tilted with his superior on every possible occasion. He condemned the appointment of Charles Bruce as the Superintendent of the Government's first tea-garden. (Wallich had heartily recommended him.) He mocked at Wallich's denigration of the climate of Assam. 'I may observe that the idea of the extreme insolubrity of Upper Assam is totally unfounded, at least so far as Europeans are concerned, and has originated from persons of timid habits in whose eyes blades of grass are death-bearing Toorais.'

It was not a happy party. But gardens were selected and the great experiment went ahead. Rather than from the official reports, which as indicated were acrimonious and contradictory, I prefer to quote from a Mr W. Nassau Lees, LL.D. who wrote a book in Calcutta in 1853. He seems hardly the impartial recorder he claims to be, but he is pretty good.

'Mr Gordon had no sooner returned to Calcutta than it was found he had been recalled at the moment his services on the spot were most required; and he was deputed a second time to China to superintend the arrangements he had made for securing supplies of trees and plants. In both his missions Mr Gordon sent round to Calcutta several casks of seeds, some plants, and eight or ten Chinamen. From the seeds about 42,000 plants were reared, which were distributed as follows:

Madras Presidency	2,000
Assam	20,000
North West Himalayas	20,000
	42,000

'The plants sent to Madras for distribution were planted at Coorg, Mysore, the Neelghiri Hills, and the Horticultural Gardens at Madras. Their story is soon told. Six months after they arrived (22 August 1836), the Chief Secretary reported to the Supreme Government "That the experiment had completely failed; and that with the exception of a few plants on the Neelghiri Hills and in the Nugger country the rest had withered away".'

Dr Lees passes over the fate of the plants sent to the Himalayas. Of the 20,000 sent to Assam, the area which had proved that it could grow tea, this is his report. 'They were sent up in boats in the care of a sergeant. When they reached Assam 8,000 only were living . . . I will here trace the progress of these unfortunate plants.'

Germinated in shade they were planted out in the full sun, which wilted them. They were in clearings, of course, but the jungle is quick to counter-attack. The ground was not kept hoed – labour was a problem from the start – and the few surviving plants were soon drowned under a rising tide of weeds. It appeared that the buffer state of north-east India had successfully resisted a Chinese invasion.

In fact, the vegetable battle was to have a most surprising end. But at present we are concerned with human endeavour. Dr Wallich might say of Charles Bruce that he was 'eminently qualified for the duties in question'; Griffiths that he was one who 'was brought up to a seafaring life and whose long residence in Assam had been devoted entirely to mercantile pursuits and the command of gun-boats'. But Bruce was a persistent pioneer, strong as a buffalo and ingenious as Robinson Crusoe. He had, besides, the gift for making friends among primitive people. His great strength carried him through the jungle even at the most malarious season. He won the trust of the wild mountain tribes. He found vast areas of wild tea-trees, the leaves of which the hill people picked, cutting down the tree if it was too tall to pluck.

He reported:

'The Singphos have known and drunk the tea for many years, but they make it in a very different way from what the Chinese do. They pluck the young and tender leaves and dry them a little in the sun three successive days; others after only a little drying put them into hot pans, turn them about until quite hot, and then place them into the hollow of a bamboo, and drive the whole down with a stick, holding and turning the bamboo over a fire all the time until it is full, then tie the end up with leaves, and hang the bamboo up in some smoky place in the hut; thus prepared the tea will keep good for years. A good way farther east they dig holes in the earth, line the sides with larger leaves, boil the tea-leaves, throw away the decoction, put the leaves into the hole, which they cover over with leaves and earth, and then allow the whole to ferment; after which it is taken out, and in this manner prepared taken to market. The Singphos pretend to be great judges of tea. All this country abounds in the plant, but they are very jealous and will give no information where it is to be found, like the Muttuck people. All the Singpho territories are overrun with wood jungle, and if only the underwood was cleared they would make a noble tea country. The soil is well adapted for the plant ... The Singphos country is a fine one, but as long as that nation can get the tea-leaves from the jungles they never will cultivate the plant. The country is thinly inhabited by a sect of men who are always fighting among themselves.'

Bruce continued to create gardens in the more peaceful districts. To these he carried young plants from the jungle and, with the help of Lieutenant Charlton, tended them. While these were too young to harvest he cut back wild trees and plucked the new leaves as they sprouted. With the help of Gordon's Chinamen, who had survived when the Chinese seedlings died, he managed to manufacture the product we call

74

tea. The first eight chests sent back to London sold at prices between 16s and 34s a pound.

Everybody realized that these were fancy prices, due mainly to novelty. None the less, everyone concerned was optimistic. The thing grew wild – big as a tree, more than holding its own in the struggle for existence, without any help from man. True, Assam remained in a sorely troubled state, as she had been for six centuries, suffering barbaric raids, the rivalry of rulers, exploitation by whoever was in power, corruption, cruelty. But in 1838 the British Government took over the whole country. Thereafter, what could limit a new industry which seemed to have the Midas touch, turning a wild thing into gold?

The Government had no sooner taken on its new political responsibility than it cut down its commercial experiment. It threw the India tea industry open to private competition.

Dr Lees:

'A joint stock company, the Assam, with a nominal capital of a million sterling was projected in London (1839) for bringing the tea *forests* of Assam, as they were called, into cultivation, and soon formed. In 1840 they commenced operations on a scale of expansion in keeping with the existing idea that the profits of the undertaking would be so rapid and so enormous as to render any attempt on economy imprudent and unnecessary. Under the exciting influence of this false idea the most extravagant expenses were incurred and sanctioned; and that nothing might be wanting to promote the enterprize Government liberally transferred to the Company its Superintendent and two-thirds of its own plantations and establishments.

'But alas for the vanity of human expectations! The *soil* in one place was not selected with reference to the requirements of the plant – *labor* in another was insufficient – the *cultivation* of a third was bad – the *superintendence* in a fourth was insufficient – *ignorance* everywhere was rampant – and to crown all the tea, when manufactured, was pronounced by the London brokers to be *bad*! The Assam Company, having by the most reckless mismanagement thrown away £200,000, the whole of its called-up capital and about £20,000 more was reduced to a state of insolvency so nearly verging on bankruptcy that £20 shares were sold in the Calcutta market for less than one rupee (about 2s). It was proposed to wind up its affairs. But this catastrophe was averted by the exertions and sound advice of Mr H. de Mornay.

75

On visiting the plantations this gentleman found them so choked with weeds that not a single plant was visible. Large sowings had been regularly made, but unfortunately had as regularly been suffered to be destroyed by the jungle and rank vegetation which springs up in Assam with magic rapidity. The company's capital had literally been poured out upon the earth and then allowed to rot. . . .

'In the meantime Government, having performed its task, and finding its only remaining garden a very unprofitable and expensive affair, sold it for a song to a Chinaman, and left the field altogether to private speculators. Now it might naturally be supposed that if anyone would succeed with *tea* a Chinaman was *the* man; but in this case it was not so. Among, for that was his name, most signally failed, and shortly after resold his bargain for half the purchase money Rs 475 (£47 10s)!

'The prospects of tea in Assam, so high at the commencement, were dimmed almost to extinction. . . .'

A scapegoat had to be found. Bruce was sacked in 1846. Not until 1847 did the tide begin to turn. In the next year, for the first time, a profit was made. It must not be supposed that throughout eight years the shareholders had remained mute. They had bitterly complained, and been scarcely appeased by small dividends paid out of capital. But when the company began to make profits the directors began to get tough and to plough back the little they made until they could genuinely afford to reward their backers.

In the Great Exhibition of 1851 the Assam Company's teas were displayed, and won the Prize Exhibition Medal. The Himalaya, Nilgiris and other Indian plantations were slower to prosper, but gradually they began together to make India the greatest tea-exporting country in the world, displacing China because China was not much interested in trade and in any case wanted most of her tea for herself.

III

Dr Wallich's last recorded act in India was doctoring, with the help of the Chinese whom Gordon had collected from southern China, the first and famous batch of Assam tea which, having been gathered from a wide area and over a considerable

76

period, reached Calcutta in a mouldy condition – and yet was sold in London so successfully. After that he went to England where he ended his dignified days.

He left behind him in the minds of men in authority his conviction that the best tea came from the hills in the north of China. Robert Fortune was sent to gather plants, seeds and knowledge.

Fortune was a character whom one immediately recognizes. As Peter Mundy was the eternal traveller, inquirer, diary writer; so Fortune was the compulsive collector. Browsing in the British Museum Library I came on catalogues of the things he had collected. They were up for sale after his death, a museum full of Oriental curiosities. He introduced heaven knows how many exotic plants and trees to England. He was the obvious choice of agent to gather specimens in an unfriendly land.

What is most fascinating to me about Fortune's books is that although he was all the time conscious of being engaged on an adventure, that adventure was for him the finding and collecting of things. Hardships, difficulties, dangers were incidental. If he had lived in an age of antique shops and nursery gardens he would have written almost as well. It just so happened, fortunately, that he was in China, travelling disguised as a Chinaman in the forbidden interior or taking his chance on the coast. In either case he went his collector's way – an educated, assured, early Victorian gentleman – putting 'a bold face on it' whenever he found himself in tiresome difficulties.

His first journey to China was made in 1843 to collect for the London Horticultural Society. His long wanderings about the Empire left him tired and weak, and on returning to the coast he went down with fever. In this state he arranged that he, with some of his most valuable specimens, should be carried south by a small native passenger boat. He was in his cot when captain and pilot hurried below to tell him that five pirate junks were bearing down on them. At first he disbelieved the news, but at last he considered it prudent to be prepared for the worst.

'I got out of bed ill and feverish as I was, and carefully examined my fire-arms, cleaning the nipples of my gun and pistols, and putting on fresh caps. I also rammed down a ball on

77

top of each charge of shot in my gun, put a pistol in each side-pocket and patiently waited for the result. By the aid of a small pocket telescope I could see as the nearest junk approached that the deck was crowded with men; I then no longer had any doubts regarding her intentions. The pilot, an intelligent old man, now came up to me and said that he thought resistance was of no use; I might manage to beat off one junk, or even two, but I had no chance with five of them. Being at the time in no mood to take advice or be dictated to by anyone I ordered him off to look after his own duty.'

Meanwhile the captain and native passengers were pulling up the boards of the cabin floor and hiding their valuables among the ballast. The common sailors hid their copper cash and all put on their very worst clothes, for the poorer a man looked, the less likely were the pirates to hold him to ransom. The only preparation for defence made by the crew was to bring up baskets of stones small enough to be thrown.

The nearest junk, when about 250 yards distant, put down her helm, swung round and fired a broadside. The shots fell short. But they cleared the decks except for the men at the helm, whom Fortune kept at this post by threatening them with his pistol. The captain, the other passengers and the rest of the crew were not seen at all during the action which followed.

The pirate junk got back upon her course and was soon overtaking again. Her second broadside fell just under the bow. The third skimmed the heads of the three men still on deck. 'The pirates now seemed quite sure of their prize, and came down upon us looking and yelling like demons. . . . This was a moment of intense interest,' Fortune writes.

When, at thirty yards' range, the junk turned sideways to fire a last broadside Fortune shouted to the helmsmen to fall flat on their faces, and did the same himself. The shots splintered the wood around them.

Then:

'I raised myself above the high stern of one junk; and while the pilots were not more than twenty yards from us, hooting and yelling, I raked their decks fore and aft with shot and ball from my double-barrelled gun. . . .

'They could not have been more surprised. Doubtless many were wounded and probably some killed. At all events the whole crew, not fewer than forty or fifty men, disappeared in a marvellous manner.'

Now the second junk came up, firing as the first had done. Again Fortune waited until she was within twenty yards, then shot down the helmsman and wounded several of the crew. There was one more attack, rather half-hearted, then all five pirate junks turned away.

As soon as this was reported the crew of Fortune's boat came rushing up from below, 'hooting and yelling as the pirates had done before' and threw stones and challenges at the retreating junks. Fortune went back to his sick-bed.

The next afternoon he was called up again to see six junks sweeping towards them from the shelter of an island. This time he tried to bluff the pirates by disguising some of the crew as Europeans in his spare clothes and arming them with bits of wood which looked like guns. But the plan had no chance of success for these men went below with the rest when the first broadside was fired, and Fortune had to revert to his original method of defence. Thus he kept them off until darkness came and they were able to escape.

'The fever which I had scarcely felt during all this excitement now returned with greater violence and I was heartily glad to go below and turn into my own bed.'

The form of gratitude shown by captain and crew was the expressed determination to carry him with them to the end of their own voyage instead of landing him at Chusan as originally arranged. But again he put a bold face on it and showed his weapons. 'This threat had the desired effect; and the trembling varlets landed me safely at Chusan.'

This last phrase suggests that Fortune had little respect for the Chinese. That may have been true on the coast. But it was entirely otherwise inland where the villagers had never seen a foreigner and were fascinated to discover that he put food into his mouth to eat as they did. These people he greatly admired for their simple friendliness, their industry, their health of mind and body. He made friends with farmers, fishermen, monks and scholars, all he met. That to a large extent was the secret of his success.

Fortune's second and most important visit to China was

made between 1848–51. He was commissioned by the East India Company to collect tea-seeds, plants and cultivators from the best inland districts. Only the best would do. 'It was well known,' he writes, 'that a variety of tea-plant existed in the southern parts of China from which inferior teas only were made. That, being more easily procured than the fine northern varieties, from which the great mass of the best teas are made, was the variety originally sent to India (by Gordon). From it all those in the Government plantations have sprung.'

To reach the Mecca of tea he had to go disguised. At the start of the journey a coolie shaved his head. 'He did not shave, he actually scraped my poor head until the tears came running down my cheeks and I cried out with pain. All he said was "Hai-yah, very bad, very bad", and continued the operation.'

Fortune's Chinese was not good enough to pass unnoticed, yet he managed to escape too much suspicion by claiming to be a traveller from a distant province of the Empire, 'beyond the Great Wall'.

None the less he often got into trouble. In the middle of the forbidden town of Hang-Chow his chair-bearers put him down and would go no farther. His personal servants had vanished.

'The position in which I was placed was rather critical. Had it been known that a foreigner was in the very heart of the city of Hang-Chow-Foo a mob would have soon collected and the consequences might have been serious.

'"Take things coolly and never lose your temper" should be the motto of every man who attempts to travel in China. This is always the best plan, for, if you allow things to take their course, ten to one you will get out of a dilemma like that in which I was now placed.'

He kept quiet, proffered money, was carried on – towards a 'Hong-la', the bearers said. 'But what a Hong-la was, was beyond my comprehension.' It proved to be an inn frequented by long-distance travellers, and there eventually his servants, who carried the baggage, found him.

He travelled on in a passenger boat up a river three or four miles wide. Here he was again in danger of detection because of his lack of skill with chopsticks. But he lifted the basin almost to his mouth and 'partly sucked and partly shovelled' the stuff in.

He was suspected. There was a certain amount of 'bobly' – pidgin for trouble – but he maintained a better than Oriental calm. Soon they were among rapids, tracking the boat upstream. Fortune took advantage of this slow progress to explore the countryside. It was hard, uncomfortable travelling. When he finally left the boat he discovered that the cargo stowed under his bunk consisted of two occupied coffins.

He reached the hill of Sung-Lo where green tea was said to have originated. Later he confirmed that green tea is not derived from a plant different from that which produces black. It is only differently treated. He learned there the secret of how the seed is kept vital during winter, before spring sowing, insulated by damp sand in baskets. He collected a large quantity of seeds. He became short of money and only with difficulty got back to Ning-Po.

His next incursion into the country was made considerably farther north. He went up into the Bohea Mountains, passing on the way an endless stream of coolies who were carrying, always in single file, their heavy loads of tea towards the coast. Looking down from the pass he saw what seemed a colony of ants on the narrow road. He passed through the huge natural rock gate which separates the province of Kiang-See from Fokien, and is guarded by soldiers.

'Never in my life have I seen such a view as this, so grand, so sublime. High ranges of mountains were towering on my right and my left, while before me as far as the eye could reach the whole country seemed broken up into mountains and hills of all heights, with peaks of every form.

'While gazing in wonder and admiration on the scene my attention was arrested by a solitary pine-tree of great size, standing about a hundred yards from the gateway. Its solitary position near the pass and its great height and beautiful symmetry made it appear a most striking object. What could it be? Was it new, or did we possess it in England? Chairs, coolies and mountains were all forgotten and I believe had the guards of Celestials attempted to prevent me from going into Fokien the only boon I should have asked at their hands would have been to be allowed to go and inspect this noble pine . . . I found it to be a Japan cedar (*Cryptomeria japonica*) a tree which I had already introduced into England. . . .'

His servants told him it had been planted by an emperor.

He reached Woo-e-Shan, heart of the Bohea district, 'considered by the Chinese to be one of the most wonderful as well as one of the most sacred spots in the Empire'. It was a cluster of 1,000-foot peaks. 'Their faces are nearly all perpendicular rock. It appears as if they had all been thrown up by some great convulsion of nature to a certain height, and as if some other force had drawn the tops of the whole mass slightly backwards, breaking it up into a thousand hills.'

Fortune went on to the temple, built at the top of one of the huge rocks.

'The High Priest . . . drew out of his tobacco pouch a small quantity of Chinese tobacco, rolled it for a moment between his fingers and thumb and then presented it to me . . . I lighted my pipe and began to smoke . . . He called the boy and ordered him to bring us some tea. And now I drank the fragrant herb, pure and unadulterated on its native hills.'

Hereabouts tea grew even in inaccessible places. There was a story, however true, that monkeys harvested it. 'These animals do not like work and would not gather the leaves willingly; but when they are far up among the rocks where the tea-bushes are growing the Chinese throw stones at them; the monkeys get very angry and commence breaking off the branches of the tea-shrubs which they throw down at their assailants.'

Fortune bought a large quantity of seeds and tea-plants in this district, many from the banks of 'The stream of Nine Wanderings' where the best souchongs and pekoes were produced. He also learned much about the art of cultivating and making tea. This was the peak of his adventure, and his official interest thereafter was in getting his seeds and specimens safely back to India.

He added 12,000 plants to the Himalayan plantations, a quantity of tools and a team of highly skilful Chinese workmen. The date was 1851.

This was the scene in India in 1851. Private companies were beginning to spring up. Seed was expensive, experts hard to find. But there was plenty of land available and first experiences were proving that you did not have to be born a Chinaman to grow and manufacture tea. The age-old mystery had been exploded. Britons could make it.

At the Great Exhibition in London people paused for a moment at the Assam stall and were mildly gratified at this further proof of British enterprise, British skill which could achieve as much in about fifteen years as the Chinese in fifteen centuries. Tea-making machinery, saving much labour, had begun to be invented. In India, subalterns and junior officials went off on leave, rode up into the hills with a dozen or more servants looking after their baggage, their meals, their camping arrangements. Some of them wandered round the tea-gardens. How gentlemanly and easy it looked! . . . Before each of these young men loomed the spectre of early retirement – life in England where living was deuced expensive and competition keen. But here, surely, was a possible alternative.

One of them wrote:

'To those (and the class is numerous in England), who, possessing but a moderate sum of money, wish nevertheless to maintain the position in life to which they have been educated, to whom trade and the professions are obnoxious, who having no military tastes or nautical tendencies are still anxious to use the energy and enterprise which are said to belong to the British – to such tea-planting offers particular inducements.'

He described the pleasant, out-of-doors occupation of supervising the growing, and how simple was the theory of manufacture:

'The newly picked leaves are forthwith bruised and left in a heap for about twenty-four hours. That the process should cause discoloration of the leaves by rupture of the small sap vessels and cells will not be a matter of surprise to any reflecting individual who, having studied the intimate connection between the vegetable and animal kingdoms, may have observed the result of violent contact with a hard body on his own anatomy.'

Work on a tea-garden, he concluded, left plenty of time for leisure and long absences. Tea was 'a property safe against the many ills that other crops are liable to'. And the prospects of making money were excellent. Given a little capital to start with it was practically impossible to fail. It was not always physically healthy, of course. Some planters sought their fortune in the jungle. But the resultant fever was naturally treated as a joke – when writing of it:

> 'It comes creeping up a fellow's back like a ton of wild cats, goes creeping through his joints like iron spikes, and is followed by a fever which prevents the patient thinking of anything save Greenland's Icy Mountains. It isn't the now-and-again kind, but gets up with a fellow at daylight and sleeps in the small of his back at night. His teeth feel about six inches long, his joints wobble like a loose waggon wheel and the shakes are so steady that he cannot hold a conversation except by putting in dashes. Then perhaps he gets better and goes on making his fortune; then he gets worse and goes on digging his grave. . . .'

But surely that sort of thing was better than poverty or an office job. Thus throughout a decade there grew up among out-of-door men the thought that if all else failed they could manage a tea-garden. Parallel with this, among the stock exchange gamblers in Calcutta and London it became the smart thing to buy up land for tea cultivation at almost any price. In the first half of the 1860s the two sides got together.

The amateur managers, no others being available, were put in charge of the generally bad and expensive land. The result was a repetition of the youthful follies of the first private venture, the Assam Company, but on a vastly greater scale. In the aggregate millions of pounds were involved. Colonel Edward Money summed up in 1870:

> 'Had managers with some practice in agriculture been chosen the end would not have been so disastrous. But anyone – literally anyone – was taken, and tea-planters in those days were a strange medley of retired or cashiered army and navy officers, medical men, engineers, veterinary surgeons, steamer captains, chemists, shopkeepers of all kinds, stable-keepers, used-up policemen, clerks, and goodness knows who besides . . . In those fever days, with the auction system, lands almost always sold for above their value. The most absurd prices, Rs 10 (£1) and upwards per

acre were sometimes paid for wild jungle lands ... weeds in all plantations were ahead of labour ... sloping land, often the steepest that could be found ... the cost of tea-seed, this item of seed alone involved enormous outlay ... It was, however, a source of great profit to the old plantations, and principally accounts for the large dividends paid for years by the Assam Company.'

Thousands directly concerned lost all they had. No one knows how many small investors at home were broken. The tea-fever very nearly killed the young industry.

Fact is stranger than fiction and so should make more interesting reading. But fact has the crudest ideas about dramatic climax. You have read the romantic story of how the Indian Princess Camellia (her other name as yet unknown) was found blushing, unscientifically recognized, in the wild jungles of Assam, of how emissaries went forth and searched through China for a prince of the highest lineage who would share her modest realm and thus raise her in the eyes of the world. Prince after prince languished after leaving China, died and had to be replaced. But the ultimate survivors perked up most surprisingly and impregnated all the native plants within reach.

There is no cure for hybridization except extermination. And the experts are now convinced that the simple Indian plant was of much the better class. The Chinese princeling, no good away from home, weakened her pure, strong blood. She could travel, but not he. The couple will certainly live happily ever after in their vegetable way. No one can stop them. But those financially interested continue even now to describe this marriage arranged with such difficulty and final triumph as the curse of the Tea Industry.

This chapter must have a better ending. Let us look farther south, at Ceylon. That island suffered not at all in the Indian tea bubble of 1860–4. Its money was in coffee, and the industry was on the up and up.

Coffee-plants had been introduced to Ceylon by the Arabs very much earlier – before the arrival of the Portuguese, who preceded the Dutch. The native Singhalese had forgotten – if they ever knew – the real value of coffee-trees. They used the young leaves to flavour their curries and the delicate jasmine-like flowers to decorate their shrines of Buddha.

In 1740 the Dutch began cultivating the coffee-trees for coffee-beans. But they made their plantations in low-lying ground, and they were not successful. It was only when the British took over and opened up communication with the inland hills that coffee production leaped ahead until it was not only the major industry of the island but the only one of any value. The virgin forests of the Kandy area provided the best land.

Some Assam tea-seeds from Dr Wallich's Botanic Gardens in Calcutta were sent to Ceylon and plants grown from them in the Botanic Gardens in Peradeniya. This was of purely academic interest. Maurice Worms brought back some cuttings from a voyage to China. These, in 1841, were planted on the Rothschild coffee estate in the Pussellawa district. Some tea was manufactured from them at a cost of a guinea a pound. This was mildly interesting as a rich man's experiment. In 1866 Arthur Morice, an experienced coffee-planter, was sent by the Governor to inspect the tea-gardens of Assam. He returned with a full report. But no one took much notice. Everybody was too busy making his fortune in coffee. Land which ten years earlier had cost about £1 an acre was selling for as much as £28 an acre – and still it paid. In 1869 there were 176,000 acres of coffee land producing per acre a quarter of a ton of beans and a profit of £5 – £8. So the coffee boom continued, cultivation extending upwards along new roads which recently had been the pilgrim paths of Adam's Peak. The plantations climbed to 5,500 feet above sea level.

By 1877 cultivation had increased to 275,000 acres. The planters were doing very well indeed. They deserved to, for they had worked extremely hard to achieve this end.

Then came disaster.

Every now and then we are awed by a display of Nature's devastating armaments – earthquakes, cyclones, eruptions, floods. But it was a microscopic organism floating in the air which ruined thousands of people and changed the whole economy of an island almost the size of England.

In a remote corner of one of the youngest districts, orange-coloured blotches appeared on the lower side of some coffee-leaves. The leaves fell and the trees affected produced fewer beans. The disease spread to other districts but for some years caused only a slight deterioration in the crops. The planters, little worried, tried to combat it by better cultivation, and meanwhile went on expanding.

Dr George Thwaites of the Royal Gardens at Peradeniya raised his voice in warning. This thing was unknown to science. It must be destroyed by fire, at any cost, before it spread further. But the planters took no notice.

A series of highly favourable seasons concealed the loss caused by the mould. At the same time the market price of coffee rose until it had gone up by nearly fifty per cent.

Meanwhile *Hemeleia vastatrix* spread at a rapidly increasing rate. Infected leaves fell from the trees, never to be replaced. The only large industry in the island died. The best use for the trees was to cut them down and send their timber to England to be made into legs for tea-tables.

The planters, so recently prosperous, were ruined. Many left the island together with the Tamil labourers. Some of those who remained made a desperate attempt to recover their fortunes by growing chinchona. Quinine sold at over Rs 11 an ounce. Then the price dropped to less than Rs 1 an ounce, and it was no longer worth taking the bark off the trees.

It seems strange, perhaps, that the planters did not earlier think of trying tea. But by that time few of them could afford to buy seeds. Those who could planted them between the rows of dead coffee-trees. The weary, discouraged men rolled up their sleeves again. And the climate was just right. . . . In 1891 a parcel of Ceylon tea was sold in Mincing Lane for £25 10s a pound. The seed of Assam had proved that *it* could travel.

Since then tea has travelled far and wide. Outside eastern and south-eastern Asia it has been cultivated on a commercial scale in Russian Transcaucasia, Natal, Nyasaland, Kenya, Uganda, and on a small scale in Thailand and Burma. It has been grown in many European countries, including England. It has been tried on islands – Borneo, the Philippines, Fiji, Mauritius,

Jamaica, Cayenne, Puerto Rico. In the Americas it has only done well in Brazil. It was experimented with in South Carolina for twenty-five years. But it did not pay. Costs were too high. Tea could only be plucked by hand, and American hands were much more expensive than those of Oriental ladies.

CHAPTER VI

Friends and Enemies

The liquid doctors rail at, and that I
Will quaff inspite of them, and when I die
We'll toss up who died first of drinking tea.
P. B. Shelley

It is with the tragic loss of the first British
Empire that tea will always be most closely
associated in the eighteenth century.
Gervas Huxley

WHILE it was still the latest thing, leaders of fashion *had* to drink tea. But it is doubtful that they liked it. Often it must have been quite nasty, stale from months or years of travel and storage, too often adulterated, and in any case brewed at first in bulk and kept in barrels to be drawn off and heated up as required. None of the early writers on tea speak of it *tasting* good.

The question was did it *do* one good – was it a panacea or a poison? That was the argument, but what imbued this argument with so much heat was that tea had been greeted as an aristocrat. It was something new and strange, an exotic famous in the East which arrived with a beautiful retinue of china and lacquer, breathing an aroma of lands more distant and romantic than those where coffee grew. Coffee in any case, from the social point of view, had quickly been segregated in coffee houses which were for men alone. Tea was the only beverage which women and men could drink together on equal terms and for long periods at a stretch. There was nothing improper about being a two tea pot woman as there was about being a two bottle man. The little ceremony of preparation – when the knowing knew of this – enhanced the attractiveness of tea, while its rarity and cost automatically reserved it for the upper strata of society. It is significant that almost the first importers of tea from the continent were two aristocrats, Lord Ossory and Lord Arlington. They brought home a large quantity from Amsterdam and sold it expensively among their friends. No gentleman at that time would have soiled his reputation by dabbling in commerce. Dealing in tea, it never occurred to the two noble lords, or to their friends, that they were being commercial. Tea was far above that.

And then this rare and precious thing turned up in the houses of the unworthy middle class, even of the *poor!* Thereafter the arguments, although still generally restricted to the medicinal merit or demerit of tea, were heated by a boiling sense of social outrage. Tea was a fallen idol, a renegade status symbol.

Before this happened Thomas Garway followed his original announcement of 1658 with a broadsheet in 1660 extolling the virtues of tea, as follows:

'The Drink is declared to be most wholesome, preserving in perfect health until extreme Old Age.
'The particular virtues are these:
'It maketh the Body active and lusty.
'It helpeth the Head-ach, giddiness and heaviness thereof.
'It removeth the Obstructions of the Spleen.
'It is very good against the Stone and Gravel, cleansing the Kidneys and Uriters being drunk with Virgin's Honey instead of sugar.
'It taketh away the difficulty of breathing, opening Obstructions.
'It is good against Lipitude, Distillations, and cleareth the sight.
'It removeth Lassitude, and cleareth and purifieth adult Humors and a hot Liver.
'It is good against Crudities, strengthening the weakness of the Ventricle or Stomack, causing good Appetite and Digestion, and particularly for Men of corpulent Body and such as are the great eaters of Flesh.
'It vanquisheth heavy Dreams, easeth the Brain, and strengtheneth the Memory.
'It overcometh superfluous Sleep, and prevents Sleepiness in general, a draught of the Infusion being taken, so that without trouble whole nights may be spent in study without hurt to the

Body, in that it moderately heateth and bindeth the mouth of the stomach.

'It prevents and cures Agues, Surfets and Feavers, by infusing a fit quantity of the Leaf, thereby provoking a most gentle Vomit and breathing of the Pores, and hath been given with wonderful success.

'It (being prepared and drank with Milk and Water) strengtheneth the inward parts, and prevents consumption, and powerfully assuageth the pains of the Bowels, or griping of the Guts or Looseness.

'It is good for Colds, Dropsies and Scurveys, if properly infused purging the Blood of Sweat and Urine, and expelleth Infection.

'It driveth away all pains in the Collick proceeding from Wind, and purgeth safely the Gall.

'And that the Virtues and Excellencies of this Leaf and Drink are many and great is evident and manifest by the high esteem and use of it (especially in later years) among the Physicians and knowing men of *France, Italy, Holland* and other parts of Christendom: and in England it had been sold in the Leaf for six pounds, and sometimes for ten pounds the pound weight, and in respect of its former scarceness and dearness, it hath been only used at *Regalia* in high Treatments and Entertainments, and Presents made thereof to Princes and Grandees till the year 1657. The said *Thomas Garway* did purchase a quantity thereof, and first publickly sold the said *Tea* in Leaf and Drink, made according to the directions of the most knowing Merchants and Travellers into Eastern Countries: And upon knowledge and experience of the said *Garway's* continued care and industry in obtaining the best *Tea*, and making Drink thereof, very many Noblemen, Physicians, Merchants and Gentlemen of Quality have ever since sent to him for the said Leaf and daily resort to his House in *Exchange Alley* aforesaid to drink the Drink thereof. ...

'And to the end that all Persons of Eminency and Quality, Gentlemen and others, who have occasion for *Tea* in Leaf may be supplied. These are given notice that the said *Thomas Garway* hath *Tea* to sell from sixteen to fifty Shillings the pound.'

Dr Cornelius Brontekoë of the University of Leyden found still more to say on the same subject, and his writings were read far beyond the borders of his native land. He liked alcoholic drinks, but the trouble was that you suffered if you drank too much of them. With tea there was no such objection. You could go on swallowing it to the limits of your capacity. As a possible maximum he mentioned two hundred cups a day. Tea, he said, warmed the stomach and stimulated the desire to study, evaporating the melancholy humours. Brontekoë picked up Garway's point, and elaborated on it, that tea overcomes superfluous sleep. In those vigorous days the desire was to go on living and learning, not to submit to – far less court – the nightly little death. Tea encouraged long profitable hours with friends or books instead of lying like a corpse on a bed. It was better for the schoolboy than the cane.

There were many who took an opposite view. A certain Dame Dorothy Bradshaigh, who founded an almshouse named 'The Receptacle', forbade the drinking of tea within its doors. 'Those who can afford to indulge themselves in an article so unnecessary, so expensive, so destructive of both time and health (the tea such people drink being poison), I shall not allow to be proper objects of Charity.'

William Cobbett denounced 'the troublesome and pernicious habit of tea drinking' for medical-cum-economic reasons. Tea had supplanted the cottager's home-brewed beer, with disastrous results. 'Can any good labourer look back on the past thirty years of his life without cursing the day when tea was first introduced into England?' Tea, Cobbett asserted, possessed 'corrosive, gnawing and poisonous powers'. It was a 'destroyer of health, an enfeebler of the frame, and engenderer of effeminacy and laziness, a debaucher of youth and a maker of misery for old age'. He made this challenge: 'Put it to the test on a lean hog, give him fifteen bushels of malt and he will repay you in ten score of bacon; but give him 730 messes of tea, and nothing else, and at the end of about seven days he is dead with hunger.'

The most responsible enemy of tea – for fiscal, not medical, reasons – was Lord President Duncan Forbes, who as Lord Advocate was concerned in remedying the effects of the Porteous riot. He was a long-nosed, dour-faced Scottish jurist who said or wrote nothing he had not carefully weighed. He put down most of the things wrong with the economy to excessive addiction to that 'most mischievous drug'. Since high duties had failed – through smuggling – to act as a deterrent he proposed that tea should be made illegal for all persons with an income of less than £50 or £100. He elaborated – a penalty of twenty shillings for a first offence, forty for a second, and so on. All servants should be forbidden tea.

He had no similar objection to alcohol. At his mother's funeral he and the guests reached the cemetery to discover that – as he put it in his memoirs – the main thing was lacking. They had left the corpse behind.

Medical criticism of tea came from the Scottish physician, Dr Thomas Short, who said that it threw some people into vapours. A religious objector was John Wesley. The Buddhist monks had advocated tea as an alternative to alcohol. Wesley, although one of his chief enemies was alcohol when his poor flock could afford this escape from sordid reality, was not so compromising. Tea was for them an extravagance. For the almost poor it meant money wasted instead of being used for better causes. For the rich it was a needless indulgence. Yet he was himself a tea-drinker in his youth, preferring it to beer at breakfast. He was a man of immense physical energy. On his seventy-second birthday he considered why it was that he should be as strong as ever, his eyesight better and his nerves firmer than they had been thirty years before. He put it down to always rising at four, generally preaching at five and never travelling less than 4,500 miles in a year. He felt that, preaching complete abstinence, he ought himself to give up tea. His experience was not unlike that of a smoker cutting out tobacco. 'The first three days my head ached, more or less, all day long, and I was half asleep from morning to night. The fourth day my memory failed, almost entirely. In the evening, I sought my remedy in prayer; and next morning my headache was gone, and my memory was as strong as ever.'

Thus strengthened he recommended to others that 'if they used English herbs instead of tea, they might hereby not only lessen their pain but in some degree their poverty'. He exhorted his flock to use the money spent on tea to buy food and clothing for the poor. We are told that about 100 London Methodists gave up tea entirely, and a large number of others undertook to be 'temperate' and drink less than previously.

Wesley maintained his own temperance for twelve years. But, being ill, tea was prescribed by his doctor. He finished his life the owner of a half gallon tea pot.

A formidable non-religious opponent was Jonas Hanway.

In his youth he had been a still more adventurous traveller than Peter Mundy. He had traded in St Petersburg, travelled in Persia, been robbed, made captive, shipwrecked, almost died of fever in the wildest quarters of the world. In middle age he was notorious for his long-winded anecdotes, and eccentric in his habit of carrying an umbrella long before fashion accepted it. He was a philanthropist who did much for outcast women and little boy chimneysweeps, the governor of a foundling hospital. And he attacked tea in a book-long essay, describing it as a 'many-headed monster which devours so great a part of the best fruits of this land'. He conceded that 'if the choice tea of China was drank only in small quantities, not hot nor strong, and confined to the higher orders of the people, it could do no great mischief'. He took it for granted there was one law for the rich and another for the poor.

'It is the curse of this nation that the labourer and mechanic will ape the Lord; and therefore I can discover no way of abolishing the use of tea unless it be done by the irrefutable force of example. It is an epidemical disease; if any seeds of it remain it will engender a universal infection.

'To what a height of folly must a nation be arrived when the common people are not satisfied with wholesome food at home, but must go to the remotest regions to please a vicious palate! There is a certain lane near Richmond where beggars are often seen in the summer season drinking their *tea*. You may see labourers who are mending the roads drinking their tea; it is even drank in cinder-carts; and what is no less absurd sold out of cups to haymakers. He who should be able to drive three Frenchmen before him, or she who might be a breeder of such a race of men are to be seen sipping their tea!

> Was it the breed of such as these
> That quell'd the proud Hysperides?

'Were they the sons of tea-sippers who won the fields of Cressy and Agincourt or dyed the Danube's streams with Gallic blood? What will be the end of such effeminate customs extended to those persons who must get their bread by the labours of the field!'

Dr Johnson reviewed Hanway's book in the *Literary Magazine*. He started in great form:

'We shall now endeavour to follow him regularly through all his observations on this modern luxury; but it can scarcely be candid not to make a previous declaration, that he is to expect little justice from the author of this extract, a hardened and shameless tea-drinker who has for twenty years diluted his meals with only the infusion of this fascinating plant, whose kettle has scarcely time to cool, who with tea amuses the evening, with tea solaces the midnight, and with tea welcomes the morning.'

The sonorous prose rolls on. But as it does so, criticism of Jonas Hanway becomes less forthright and the praise of tea more qualified. It is as if the doctor were a little self-conscious about his addiction to the drink. 'As it neither exhilarates the heart, nor stimulates the palate, it is commonly an entertainment purely nominal, a pretence for assembling to prattle, for interrupting business, or diversifying idleness.'

And at the end Johnson shows that he is much of a mind with Hanway in the matter of the two laws.

'I have no desire to appear captious, and shall therefore readily admit, that tea is a liquor not proper for the lower classes of the people, as it supplies no strength to labour, or relief to disease, but gratifies the taste without nourishing the body. It is a barren superfluity to which those who can hardly procure what nature requires, cannot prudently habituate themselves. Its proper use is to amuse the idle, and relax the studious, and dilute the full meals of those who cannot use exercise, and will not use abstinence.'

Hanway answered Johnson's criticisms, and Johnson – for the only occasion of his life, according to Boswell – 'condescended to oppose anything that was written against him'. He answered the answer. But it is all rather unsatisfactory as arguments about taste are bound to be.

As for the exaggerated medical claims and warnings, these were settled for good in 1772 by the most successful, if not the most respected, doctor of his day, John Cookly Lettsom. He was born of a Quaker family in the Virgin Islands and came to England at the age of six. Having in due course qualified as a doctor he returned to the West Indies and in practice there made £2,000 in six months. On the strength of this he set up in London. Thereafter he went from strength to strength, earning it has been said £12,000 a year, an enormous salary at that time. He always wore the Quaker dress which must have added a solemn dignity to his bedside manner.

He was a prolific letter-writer and author, producing works on medicine, on biographical and philanthropic subjects. Nearly all his writing was done in his carriage while being driven on his medical rounds. To me it is always a source of wonder that a good doctor can without apparent effort pass from one private chamber of the mind and body to another, giving his whole attention for a quarter of an hour or so to each throughout the day. To sandwich creative work between these visits is surely remarkable.

Lettsom's judgement on tea showed common sense. He wrote: 'As the custom of drinking tea is become universal every person may be considered a judge of its effects, at least so far as concerns his own health.' Having examined all the evidence he concluded:

> 'Tea if not drunk too hot, nor in too great quantities, is perhaps preferable to any other vegetable infusion we know. And if we take into consideration likewise its known enlivening energy, it will appear that our attachment to tea is not merely from its being costly or fashionable, but from its superiority in taste and effect to most other vegetables.'

II

One is doubtful whether to class poets as friends or enemies of tea. When they mention it at all they are almost invariably polite – too carefully and uninspiredly so, as if speaking of a good but ugly woman. With few exceptions it is only the lesser ones who poetize about it. But it is a word

> Which Pope himself would sometimes condescend
> To place commodious at a couplet's end,

and thereby show how it was pronounced:

> Here thou, great Anna, whom two realms obey
> Dost sometimes council take, and sometimes tea.

He does the same for Bohea which was then synonymous with black tea:

Where the gilt chariot never marks the way,
Where none learn ombre, none e'er taste Bohea.

We know this is not poetic licence because Pope did not allow himself any. But it is wit rather than poetry.

The Chinese, judging by literal translations, were able to make quaint poetry on the subject:

The first cup moistens my lips and throat;
The second cup breaks my loneliness;
The third cup scorches my barren entrail
but to find therein some five thousand
volumes of odd ideographs;
The fourth cup raises a slight perspiration –
all the wrongs of life pour out through my pores;
At the fifth cup I am purified;
The sixth cup calls me to the realms of
the immortals.
The seventh cup – ah, but I could take no more.
I only feel the breath of the cool breeze that
passes up my sleeves.

(It is probably just as well that the poet did not, like Dr Brontekoë, drink two hundred cups.)

A few English poets, like Dean Swift, associated tea with scandal:

Surrounded with the noisy clans
Of prudes, coquettes and harridans.

Or Elizabeth Barrett Browning who described a lady who

. . . helps to sugar her Bohea at night
with your reputation.

In justice we must hear the other side. One group of ladies at least never mixed scandal with their tea. The blue-stockings, queened by Mrs Montagu, ably supported by Mrs Vesey; Hannah More, the female Maecenas of Hill Street; Miss Joanna Baillie, the female Shakespeare of her age; Miss Seward, the Swan of Lichfield; Mrs Elizabeth Carter; Mrs Chapone, and other highly educated and intelligent females met for the sole purpose of drinking tea and sharing the pleasure of 'general conversation as little disgraced by calumny, levity and the other censorable errors with which it is too commonly tainted',

as Hannah More put it. She also put it in a poem dedicated to
'Vesey, of Verse the judge and friend' and entitled 'The Bas
Bleu, or Conversation'. In the course of a good many pages she
exclaims:

> Hail Conversation, soothing Power,
> Sweet Goddess of the social hour! . . .
> Long may thy polish'd altars blaze
> With wax-lights' undiminish'd rays!
> Still be thy nightly offerings paid,
> Libations large of Lemonade.
> On silver vases, loaded, rise
> The biscuits' ample sacrifice.
> Nor be the milk-white stream forgot
> Of thirst-assuaging, cool orgeot!
> Rise, incense pure from fragrant Tea
> Delicious incense, worthy Thee! . . .
> Still may thy gentle reign extend,
> And taste and wit with science blend!
> Soft polisher of rugged man. . . .

That sort of thing kept rugged man away from the tea-
table. Byron for one was not favourably impressed:

> Oh, 'darkly, deeply, beautifully blue',
> As someone somewhere sings about the sky,
> And I, ye learned ladies, sing of you,
> They say your stockings are so – Heaven knows why.

But ladies must not by any means be considered enemies of
tea. For the most part they are worshippers. And was it not a
Duchess of Bedford – not the Duke – who invented tea, the
meal, which has meant so much to so many ever since?

Back to male poets – Edmund Waller, who could write a
thing as delicately charming as:

> Go lovely Rose –
> Tell her that wastes her time and me. . . .

was smug and silly when he wrote of tea. He addressed a birthday ode to Catherine of Braganza. No need to quote it all but:

> Venus her Myrtle, Phoebus has his bays;
> Tea both excels, which she vouchsafe to praise . . .
> The Muse's friend, tea doth our fancy aid,

Repress those vapours which the head invade.
And keep the palace of the soul serene,
Fit on her birthday to salute the Queen.

Much the best poet of tea was William Cowper who had a genuine love of tea and all it stood for:

> Now stir the fire, and close the shutters fast,
> Let fall the curtains, wheel the sofa round,
> And while the bubbling and loud-hissing urn
> Throws up a steamy column, and the cups
> That cheer but not inebriate, wait on each,
> So let us welcome peaceful evening in.

There is your cosy English tea! But cosiness is not the quality we look for in our muses. No, tea does not inspire to poetry and song although it has had a much more adventurous career than wine which starts its life by being trodden underfoot, is upset by any form of change or travel and remains bottled up until the day of its death. What tea does do is to clear creative brains and sweep away the superfluous sleep which too often smothers the small, shy, midnight flower of genius.

It has been a good friend to prose writers who, on their side, have proved far more inspired than poets to express their obligation to it. Dr Johnson, a clear thinker if there ever was one, is the best example.

Dickens was less honest. He profited by tea but mocked it in his writings, as when the young lady at the Brick Lane branch of the Grand Junction Ebenezer Temperance Association meeting caused alarm to Sam Weller after her ninth cup of tea by 'swellin' wisibly'. Thackeray paid the pretty compliment, 'Nature meant very kindly by women when she made the tea-plant.' And de Quincey, the author whom everyone has heard of and nobody has read, called tea 'the beverage of intelligence', which is as apt as it is brief.

I know of no musician who either worked on the stimulus of tea or celebrated it by a cantata, as Bach did for coffee. As for the other professions, anyone who has been in the British army knows that plenty of cha is essential to good morale – so much so that the soldier complains of its absence rather than praises its presence. Going back a bit, Garnet Wolseley, a junior officer in the Crimean War, saw to it that his hungry men at least got plenty of hot tea. The Duke of Wellington was a strong advocate of its virtues. He carried in his campaigning baggage a tea pot designed by Flaxman and made by Wedgwood to commemorate the battle of Vittoria.

The clergy almost to a man have been friends of tea – from the country parson in a poor living by the sea who felt that the end justified the means and accepted it from the smugglers, to such men of fame and later fortune as Sidney Smith. Smith disagreed entirely with the sentiment expressed in Cowper's famous line, 'God made the country, and man made the town.' He called the country 'a kind of healthy grave'. Living there for much of his life he exclaimed, 'Thank God for tea! What would the world do without tea? How did it exist? I am glad I was not born before tea!' But another divine, John Ovington, must be counted an enemy for his negative compliment: 'This admirable drink reconciles men to sobriety.'

Garrick was a friend of tea (though he did not like it strong). So was the dramatist, Richard Cumberland, and Sir Joshua Reynolds too, as they had to be, being Johnson's friends. That gives us champions from three more callings. But no one who followed the law has neutralized the attack of Lord Advocate Duncan Forbes.

With politics we bring up the big guns. Gladstone claimed that he drank more tea between midnight and 4 a.m. than any two other members of Parliament put together. He said, 'If you are cold tea will warm you – if you are heated, it will cool you – if you are depressed, it will cheer you – if you are excited, it will calm you.' As a good member of the Opposition he opposed a reduction in the duty on tea when the Conservatives proposed it, but he brought forward the same measure, and carried it, when his party came to power. Mr Balfour and M. Clemenceau brought some real peace to the Conference of Versailles by drinking tea together. Finally, there was George Washington who, we are told, 'ordinarily for breakfast had tea, English fashion'. In view of the little trouble to be covered in the next section that helps to demonstrate the clear dispassionate thinking of the first President of the United States.

To quote Dr Johnson once more: 'The love of country when it rises to enthusiasm is an ambiguous and uncertain virtue: when a man is enthusiastick he ceases to be reasonable, and when he once departs from reason what will he do but drink sour tea?'

It turned sour in the mouths of the American colonists the year after Dr Lettsom gave his judgement. They were of good tea-drinking stock, and they liked it very much for what it was. Enormous quantities were drunk in the towns. New York had a pump of pure water which was sold exclusively for tea-making. Tea-tables, much smaller and more intimate than the big communal board of other meals, began to appear in the second decade of the eighteenth century. At the huge funeral gatherings of those days the ladies at least drowned their sorrow in tea. It was brewed in the backwoods. It was drunk by the English standing army.

It was either expensive or bad. That which came from the monopolist East India Company sold at its high fixed price. The Dutch tea was cheap and poor in quality. The colonists imitated their forefathers, not only in drinking tea but also in smuggling it. No doubt there are as many fine houses built from smuggling fortunes in the United States as there are in England.

Coffee was rare, chocolate rarer. Tea was becoming more and more a part of the American way of life when the British Cabinet chose it as the commodity which they would tax to prove their right to tax the colonists. The proposed tax was nominal, 3d a pound. To a fairly heavy tea-drinker this re-presented only half a crown a year. With the English domestic duty removed it meant that good tea was as cheap as the inferior Dutch import. But it was a matter of principle. To drink the taxed article meant accepting the British Government's right to tax. Consequently the unfortunate China herb became detested tea, a symbol of oppression, rank poison, far fetched and dear bought, a base exotic and much more besides from the politician's rich store of invective.

Everybody who has been at school knows what happened when the ships carrying the taxable tea reached the Atlantic seaboard of America. But one gets an emphasis very different from that of the history books in the current English newspapers. These show that the British public remained supremely calm, more critical of their own Government than of the colonists. This is so striking that I must stress at the start that *all* the quotations are from English papers, published in London, and that they constitute *all* the Press references to the subject which can be found. As you will see, when the two sides met in Boston, Philadelphia, Charlestown and New York, they never forgot their manners. If tea was a herald of war it was a very courteous and broad-minded one.

Newspapers of the period are rarely of more than half a dozen pages. They are set solid, column after column. No space is wasted on headings, changes of subject being indicated by a few words in italics of the same type size as the rest. The first page is occupied with long letters to the editor signed by such immortals as 'Country Gentleman', Candidus' and 'Unbiassed'. Foreign news merely gives the place of origin – '*Warsaw*', '*Lower Elbe*', '*Rome*', and runs on, unbroken as a canal, until it reaches '*Bankruptcies*', '*Parliament*' and what we would call classified advertisements of cock-fighting, fine silks for sale, pills and worm cures. '*Dramatic news*' means information about the theatre.

At the height of the tea tax crisis *The Times* was not yet born, the *Morning Post* was only two years old and its relevant copies have unfortunately been lost or destroyed by enemy action. Such daily papers as existed, and of which copies are preserved, have names unknown today. It took a long and careful search of small print columns to find the items quoted below. They are given in the order in which they were written. That is rarely the same as the order of publication in England for they took anything between three and six weeks to cross the Atlantic.

The *Daily Advertiser*, 2 February 1774:

'*New York* November 1st, 1773. All America is in a Flame on account of the Tea Exportation. The New Yorkers as well as the Bostonians and Philadelphians are, it seems, determined that no tea shall be landed. They have published a Paper in Numbers called the Alarm. It begins first with "Dear Countrymen", and then goes on exhorting them to open their eyes and like Sons of

Liberty throw off all Connection with the Mother Country. They have on this Occasion raised a Company of Artillery, and every Day almost are practising at a Target. Their Independent Companies are out at exercise every day. The minds of the lower people are influenced by the example of some of their principals. They swear that they will burn every ship that comes in; but I believe our Six and Twelve Pounders with the Royal Welsh Fuziliers will prevent anything of that kind.'

The *Westminster Journal*, 29 January 1774:

'*Charles Town, South Carolina Nov. 20th.* The Tea affair makes a great noise here, but nothing is yet done; it will be prevented landing, without doubt.'

The *Daily Advertiser*, 2 February 1774:

'*New York Dec. 1st.* All is in confusion about the Tea-ships, and the Governor has now declared that he expects a ship with 400 Chests of Tea. The Artillery have orders to make up Ball Cartridges, as have the troops. Yesterday Orders were given for all soldiers to keep good Flints in their Firelocks, and every Officer and Soldier as soon as any Riot is in the Town (if there) to repair directly to the Barracks and acquaint the Commanding Officer of it. General Haldiman has got two Cohorns before his house and the Governor a stronger Guard. The Swan Sloop of War is gone down to the Watering Place to wait for the Ship to bring her up, as they have threatened all the Pilots to bring them to Liberty Tree if they conduct the Ship in. Thus affairs stand at present.'

The *Westminster Journal*, 29 January 1774:

'*New York, Dec. 6th.* The following notice has been dispersed about the City: – Whereas our nation have lately been informed, that the fetters, that have been forged for us by Great Britain, are hourly expected to arrive in a certain ship, belonging to or chartered by the East India Company: We do therefore declare, that we are determined not to be enslaved by any power on earth; and that whosoever shall aid, or abet, so infamous a design, or shall presume to lett their store, or stores, for the reception of the infernal chains, may depend upon it that we are prepared, and shall not fail to pay them an unwelcome visit, in which they shall be treated as they deserve, by

THE MOHAWKS November 29, 1773.'

An account of the actual Tea Party was printed in the *Morning Chronicle and London Advertiser* of 22 January 1774. It is on an inside page and starts near the bottom of a column, the only heading being, in small italics, 'From the Boston (New England) Gazette'. The *Gazetteer and New Daily Advertiser* and the *Westminster Journal* used the same account on 22 January and 29 January respectively. I have found in the English Press no dispatch from an English or pro-English source. Thus, not only was the incident treated as if of no particular importance, but the enemy's version was given verbatim, exclusively and without comment. This is a very strange thing to have happened – unless the Boston Tea Party was not considered at the time an important event and was only built up as such later on.

'*Boston Dec. 20th*, 1774. On Tuesday last the body of the people of this and at adjacent towns, and others from the distance of 20 miles, assembled at the Old South Meeting House to enquire the reason of the delay in sending the Ship Dartmouth with the East India tea back to London; and having found that the owner had not taken the necessary steps for that purpose, they enjoined him at his peril to demand of the collector of the Customs a clearance for the Ship, and appointed a committee of ten to see it performed; after which they adjourned to the Thursday following ten o'clock. They then met and being informed by Mr Roach that a clearance was refused him, they enjoined him immediately to make a protest and apply to the Governor for a passport by the Castle, and adjourned again till three o'clock for the same day. At which time they again met and after waiting till near sun set Mr Roach came in and informed them that he had accordingly entered his protest and waited on the Governor for a pass, but his Excellency told him he could not, consistent with his duty, grant it until his vessel was qualified. The people finding all their efforts to preserve the property of the East India Company, and return it safely to London, frustrated by the consignees, the Collector of the Customs, and the Governor of the Province, dissolved their meeting – But, behold, what followed! A number of resolute men (dressed like Mohawks or Indians) determined to do all in their power to save their country from the ruin which their enemies had plotted, in less than four hours emptied every chest on board the three ships commanded by the Captains Hall, Bruce and Coffin, amounting to 342 chests, into the sea! Without the least damage done to the ships, or any other property. The masters and owners are well pleased that their ships are thus cleared; and the people are almost universally congratulating each other on this happy event.'

There is no editorial comment whatever in any of the three papers which print this account. But another English newspaper, the *Gazetteer and New Daily Advertiser* adds, also dated 'Boston Dec 20th':

'Captain Loring in a brig from London for this place, having 58 chests of the detested tea on board, was cast ashore on the back of Cape Cod last Friday se'nnight. It is expected the Cape Indians will give us a good account of the tea against our next.

'We are positively informed, that the patriotic inhabitants of Lexington unanimously resolved against the use of Bohea tea of all sorts, Dutch or English importation; and to manifest the sincerity of this resolution they brought together every ounce contained in the town and committed it to one common bonfire.'

From the *Morning Chronicle*, 2 February 1774:

'*Boston 22 Dec.* I am sorry to assure you, that respecting our behaviour, what at first was a praise-worthy opposition, soon degenerated into an unrestrained licentiousness. The Bostonians observed no medium. Government had a certain right to give a sanction to the East India Company, which undoubtedly had a privilege under the sanction of an act of the legislative body (on which the Colonies are dependent not withstanding their boasted charters) to land the teas. A very easy remedy remained with the Colonists: they were not compelled to buy; and by restricting themselves from purchasing would have effectively overturned all the measures taken to impose on them.

'It has been given out that six regiments and some men of war are to be sent to Boston. But the better opinion is, grounded upon its being more consistent with the genius of our Court, that orders will be sent to Boston to seize the Committee men and send them over here to be tried. . . .'

From the *Daily Advertiser*, 29 January 1774:

'*Philadelphia, Dec. 27th.* On Saturday last an express came from Chester to inform the Town that the Tea Ship commanded by Captain Ayres, with her detected cargo, was arrived there, having followed another ship up the river so far.

'The Committee which had been appointed to arrange the business for preventing the landing of the tea met early the next morning, and being apprized of the arrival of Mr Gilbert Barclay, the Consignee who came passenger in the ship, they immediately went in a body to request the Renunciation of the Commission. Mr Barclay politely attended the Committee at the first Request, and being made acquainted with the sentiments of the City, and the dangers to which the public Liberties of America were exposed by this Measure, he after expressing the particular hardship of the situation, resigned the Commission in a manner which affected everyone present.

'The Committee then appointed three of their Members to go to Chester, and two to Gloucester Point, in order to have the earliest Opportunity of meeting Captain Ayres and representing to him the sense of the Publick respecting his Voyage and Cargo. The Gentlemen who had set out for Chester, receiving Intelligence that the Vessel had weighed Anchor at about Twelve o'Clock, and proceeded to Town, returned. About Two o'Clock she appeared in Sight of Gloucester Point, where a Number of Inhabitants from the Town had assembled with the Gentlemen of the Committee. As she passed along, she was hailed, and the Captain requested not to proceed further but to come on shore. This the Captain complied with, and was handed through a Lane, made by the People, to the Gentleman appointed to confer with him.

'They represented to him the general sentiments, together with the Danger and Difficulties that would attend his Refusal to comply with the wishes of the Inhabitants; and finally desired him to proceed with them to the Town, where he would be more fully informed of the Temper and Resolution of the People. He was accordingly accompanied to the Town by a number of Persons, where he was soon convinced of the Truth and Propriety of the Representations which had been made to him, and agreed that upon the Desire of the Inhabitants being publickly expressed, he would conduct himself accordingly. Some small Rudeness being offered to the Captain afterwards in the Street by some Boys, several Gentlemen interposed, and suppressed it before he received the least Injury. Upon an Hour's Notice this morning, a public Meeting was called, and the State-House not being sufficient to hold the Numbers assembled, they adjourned into the Square. This meeting is allowed by all to be the most respectable, both in the Numbers and Rank of those who attended it, that has been known in this City. After a short Introduction the following Resolutions were not only agreed to, but the public Approbation testified in the warmest Manner.

'1. Resolved, That the Tea on board the ship Polly, Captain

Ayres, should not be landed. 2. That Captain Ayres shall neither enter nor report his vessel at the Customs-House. 3. That Captain Ayres shall carry back the Tea immediately. 4. That Captain Ayres shall immediately send a pilot on board his Vessel, with Orders to take Charge of her, and proceed with her to Reedy Island next High Water. 5. That the Captain shall be allowed to stay in Town till Tomorrow, to provide Necessaries for his Voyage. 6. That he shall then be obliged to leave the Town and proceed to his Vessel, and make the best of his way out of our River and Bay. 7. That a Committee of four Gentlemen be appointed to see these Resolutions carried into Execution.

'The Assembly were then informed of the Spirit and Resolution of New York, Charles-Town, South-Carolina, and the Conduct of the People of Boston, where upon it was unanimously resolved:

'That this Assembly highly approve the Conduct and Spirit of the People of New York, Charles-Town and Boston, and return their hearty Thanks to the People of Boston for their Resolution in destroying the Tea rather than suffering it to be landed.

'The whole Business was conducted with a Decorum and Order worthy of the Importance of the Cause. Capt. Ayres being present at the Meeting, solemnly and publickly engaged that he would literally comply with the sense of the City, as expressed in the above Resolutions.

'A proper Supply of Necessaries and fresh Provisions being then procured, in about two Hours the Tea-ship weighed Anchor from Gloucester Point, where it lay within sight of the Town, and has proceeded, with her cargo, on her Return to the East India Company.

'The Publick think that the Conduct of those Gentlemen whose goods are returned on board the Tea-ship ought not to pass unnoticed, as they have on this occasion generously sacrificed their private interests to the Publick Good.'

Without any break the column continues as follows:

'*Charles-town South Carolina Dec. 5th.* Several vessels belonging to North America have been lately seized in Hispaniola.

'Tomorrow morning a Sermon will be preached on Behalf of the Charity Children of St Giles in the Fields and St George, Bloomsbury....'

Here is the first reported official reaction in England, from the *Morning Chronicle,* 31 January. 'The throwing of the tea into the sea at Boston irritated the Court extremely, and while this shews the indignity with which the legislative authority of this country is treated in America, gives room to apprehend, that if force is attempted, it will be opposed.'

An editorial comment suggests that the Government was scarcely more popular at home than it was on the other side of the Atlantic:

> 'The fate of America, and in that, of Great Britain, depends on the advice, or rather *report*, which the Privy Council shall make to the King upon this occasion. The situation of affairs in America is become more truly alarming than ever. The union throughout the continent to reject the tea, while it is subject to a duty to be paid there, shows that the Ministers, or rather the miserable Cabinet Junto in whom *only* the King thinks proper to confide, are as cordially despised in America as they are detested in England.'

From the *Daily Advertiser*, 1 February 1774:

> 'The vessels which were to sail this week laden with goods for Boston are stopped by the merchant exporters till the affair of that colony are a little more settled.
>
> 'A theatrical correspondent observes that Mr Slater merits the severest reprehension for his conduct on Saturday evening; his part in the new comedy was a very short one, and yet he was not able to recite two thirds of it in a proper manner. . . . '

From the *Morning Chronicle*, 7 February 1774:

> 'By advices from New England, of undoubted authority, we learn that the ladies throughout the four provinces have entered into a solemn agreement not to drink any tea imported from Great Britain (nor to wear any British manufactures) until the acts of Parliament imposing a duty on tea exported to America are totally repealed.'

Tea is branded a *casus belli*. From this war the United States was born.

In America tea never recovered from being thrown into the sea. But Agnes Repplier, an American, in her delightful *To Think of Tea* contends that its ill name at the time of the Revolution was by no means the only cause for its lack of popularity in the United States.

> 'Other causes brought about its downfall. When the descendants

of the English tea-drinkers were overwhelmed by heavy tides of emigration, and dwindled to so pitiful a minority that, as an immigrant author tauntingly observed, they could not swing an election, the drink of their forefathers dwindled with them. For years the Irish kept it going; but the Irish failed to hold what they had gained, and America became the great melting-pot of the world. What was the delicate distinction of tea to these massed invaders, for whom it held no significance, no pleasant memories, and no delight?'

IV

Finally among enemies of tea one must mention those who adulterated it or offered substitutes. Before tea was packaged – which was quite lately – and still more in those earliest days when it was sold in liquid form it was often scandalously doctored to cheat the revenue and the unsophisticated consumer.

Several Acts of Parliament were passed against adulterants in the eighteenth century. As for substitutes, there were a number of open and therefore innocent ones offered to the public, particularly in America after their quarrel with real tea – Liberty tea, which was made of the four-leaved loosestrife, sage tea, balsam tea, Labrador tea. There was also balm tea, and tea made from ribwort, currant leaves and holly leaves.

In the Cambridge University Library I had the luck to come upon an anonymous, undated work entitled *Tea* which goes into adulteration in fascinating detail.

But first the substitutes. Labrador tea, which I had imagined was the infusion of black spruce needles given me by the Indians in Labrador when we ran out of everything, is in fact made with *Ledum latifolium* – a shrub allied to the rhododendron: 'It is a grateful aromatic bitter and is highly salutory and invigorating.' Paraquay tea, presumably *maté*, consists of '*Cossina Paragua* and *Ilex Vomitoria* which is diuretic in infusion, and diminishes hunger; but if too much is used it becomes emetic. An infusion of high-dried leaves is drank by the Apalachians as an exhilarant.' But the French make the best substitute:

'by heating the leaves of hornbeam in a new earthen vessel placed in the middle of boiling water till they have acquired a brown

109

hue, lighter or darker at pleasure; they are then scented by being placed in a box together with the root of the Florence iris, in powder, for several days; after which they may be used for tea . . . so perfect as to deceive persons not previously informed.'

The adulterants, on the other hand, were added to the real tea to increase its bulk at small cost. The leaves of the sloe or blackthorn (which the anonymous author says are poisonous) were the most popular. The leaves were added to tea, and the juice of the berries to port wine. Before he becomes too angry, the author allows himself a pun and a rhyme. 'Wine and tea are sloe poisons. . . .'

> China and Porto now farewell
> Let others buy what you've to sell,
> Your Port and your Bohea;
> For we've our native sloe divine
> Whose fruit yields all our Porto wine,
> Whose leaves make all our tea.

The adulterant called 'smouch' was also made up of ash leaves, wheat husks, liquorice and other ingredients later to be specified. The author calculated that 4,000,000 lb were made in 1783, in which year the East India Company imported only 6,000,000 lb of genuine tea.

'When gathered they (the ash leaves) are first dried in the sun, then baked; they are next put upon a floor and trod upon until the leaves are small, then sifted and steeped in copperas and with sheep's dung; after which, being dried on a floor, they are fit for use . . . The fine quality is sold at four guineas per hundred weight, equal to ninepence per pound. The coarse is sold at two guineas a hundred weight . . . Elder buds are manufactured in some places to represent fine tea. . . .

'In Scotland and Ireland similar practices have been carried out to an equal extent, and with greater ingenuity; in the latter country the penalties imposed for this offence have during a few months amounted to more than £15,000. A Dublin newspaper of August last states the arrest of a petty farmer in the parish of Tallaght, County of Dublin, who, with two Englishmen absconded, have been actively employed in the manufacture of Tea for some of the Dublin grocers with the following materials:

'Black and Deadly Nightshade (Poison)
Ivy leaves (Poison when taken in large quantities)

Boughlan Buy (Ditto, ditto)
Robin-run-the-hedge (one of the most severe purgatives among
    our indigenous plants)
Mountain sage (rather conductive [*sic*] to health)
Two descriptions of Alder leaves (very bad)
Potato leaves, when in season (Ditto)

'These were cured by a vitriolic preparation, and coloured for green tea with verdigris – for black tea with copperas.'

The legal penalty was a fine of £10 for every pound weight of smouch made or twelve months' imprisonment. But our author did not believe this would stop a traffic which yielded 300–600 per cent profit. In fact it continued until reductions in the price of real tea made the possible profit negligible.

One is reminded of George Meredith's story of the old man seen gathering weeds in the outskirts of Brussels. When asked what he was picking he answered simply, 'Tea for the English.'

CHAPTER VII

Each to his Taste

I feel my native courage fail
To see a Gascon eat a snail;
I dare not ask abroad for tea;
No cannibal can dine with me;
And all the world is torn and rent
By varying views on nutriment.
And yet upon the other hand,
De gustibus non disputand –

                                        – um.

Hilaire Belloc

THE argument as to which should be put first into the cup, the tea or the milk, is as old and unsolvable as which came first, the chicken or the egg. There is, I think, a vague feeling that it is non-U to put the milk in first – why, goodness knows. However that may be, tea was drunk for many centuries before anyone thought of taking milk with it.

It was either the English or the French who first drank tea with milk. Thomas Garway, you remember, claimed that the inward parts were strengthened by putting milk in tea. In 1680 Madame de Sévigné wrote of a friend who put tea in her milk to take the chill off.

Incidentally it is interesting that tea should so quickly have gathered superstitions. There are none of coffee and cocoa although they reached the West earlier. But to stir tea in the pot is to stir up strife. Bubbles in your cup show that kisses are coming, but if you put in milk before the sugar (never mind about the tea) you risk losing your sweetheart. If a girl allows a man to pour out a second cup of tea for her she will succumb to his designs. (I have been unable to discover whether it works the other way round.) And of course there is the advance information given by a floating tea-leaf that a stranger is coming, the number of taps with one hand it takes to shake it off the back of the other hand showing how many days there are to wait. People who make tea with water which is not boiling must expect a lot of strangers, but if they use strainers or tea-bags they will get no warning of it. Perhaps they are afraid to face the future.

When people in England ceased buying tea by the pint from coffee houses they learned how to make it in their homes and have done so ever since. There is only one way; we practise it and the rest of the world does not, they say. Travel any summer evening in the boat-train from a channel port to London and you will hear someone say that Athens, Paris, Capri, Monte Carlo or wherever they may have been was an experience but it is nice to have a *real* cup of tea again.

One wonders what the remark might be if his – or more probably her – holiday had taken the speaker far enough afield to drink tea with some of the peoples who had brewed it a thousand years longer than we have.

In China as elsewhere tea was first drunk exclusively for its supposed medicinal qualities. It must have been nasty enough for people to believe it did them good. Fresh leaves, entirely untreated, were steeped in hot water, producing a bitter and astringent drink. Later, according to the *Kuang Yu*, a sort of dictionary published in the fifth century, it is said that the leaves were crushed into cakes, then roasted until reddish in colour and finally pounded to pieces and infused in an earthenware jar. Onion, ginger and orange were added to make it palatable. It was in the reign of an emperor of the Sui dynasty, named Wen Ti, when tea began to be drunk as a beverage. Even so herbs and salt were added to improve the flavour. Salt (not sugar) was the last extra ingredient used in the East. Since then the Chinese have drunk tea as do enlightened Westerners, neat, the only difference being that although the tea pot came from China the Chinese infuse the leaves in the individual cups – not at all a bad way of doing it.

In the *Ch'a Ching*, as has been said, Lu Yu set down a code of tea-drinking behaviour. Something so nearly holy might well have become surrounded by a complicated ritual in China. But the barbaric Tartars put a stop to that. Even so tea became an essential ingredient of both hospitality and business – as it almost is in England.

It was left to the Japanese to develop the tea ceremony to its illogical conclusion. Everything is symbolic of something else. The tea-room is a place apart, approached by a path which, however short, represents an escape from the troubled world. The door is only three feet high so the room is entered in the attitude of humility. The room is small and without ornaments – except for symbolically arranged flowers – to encourage simplicity and peace. Periods of silence or of a prescribed form of conversation are required. The tea is prepared just so and drunk just so while seated cross-legged on a mat, every movement being significant. It is said to take three years to perfect this ritual, far, far more complicated than wine-tasting. After drinking, the host deprecates the tea, saying how poor it is. A Westerner would be inclined to agree with him, for it is in fact tea-powder whisked up into something reminiscent of pea soup with a thing like a shaving brush made of finely split bamboo. When it is all over the host kneels at the door, bowing his head in humble gratitude for the polite expressions of his departing guests.

Okakura-Kakuzo explains the purpose of the ceremony in these words:

'In religion the future is behind us. In art the present is the eternal. The tea-masters held that the real appreciation of art is only possible to those who make of it a living influence. Thus they sought to regulate their daily life by the high standard of refinement which obtained in the tea-room. In all circumstances serenity of mind should be maintained, and conversation should be so conducted as never to mar the harmony of the surroundings.'

As an example of the serenity achieved by this means one may read his description of the last tea of Rikiu.

'Long had been the friendship between Rikiu and the Taiko-Hideyoshi, and high the estimation in which the great warrior held the tea-master. But the friendship of a despot is ever a dangerous honour. It was an age rife with treachery, and men trusted not even their nearest kin. Rikiu was no servile courtier, and had often dared to differ in argument with his fierce patron.

Taking advantage of the coldness which had for some time existed between the Taiko and Rikiu, the enemies of the latter accused him of being implicated in a conspiracy to poison the despot. It was whispered to Hideyoshi that the fatal potion was to be administered to him with a cup of the green beverage prepared by the tea-master. With Hideyoshi suspicion was sufficient ground for instant execution, and there was no appeal from the will of the angry ruler. One privilege alone was granted to the condemned – the honour of dying by his own hand.

'On the day destined for his self-immolation, Rikiu invited his chief disciples to a last tea-ceremony. Mournfully at the appointed time the guests met at the portico. As they look into the garden path the trees seem to shudder, and in the rustling of their leaves are heard the whispers of homeless ghosts. Like solemn sentinels before the gates of Hades stand the grey stone lanterns. A wave of rare incense is wafted from the tea-room; it is the summons which bids the guests to enter. One by one they advance and take their places. In the tokonoma hangs a kakemono – a wonderful writing by an ancient monk dealing with the evanescence of all earthly things. The singing kettle, as it boils over the brazier, sounds like some cicada pouring forth his woes to departing summer. Soon the host enters the room. Each in turn is served with tea, and each in turn silently drains his cup, the host last of all. According to established etiquette, the chief guest now asks permission to examine the tea-equipage. Rikiu places the various articles before them with the kakemono. After all have expressed admiration of their beauty, Rikiu presents one of them to each of the assembled company as a souvenir. The bowl alone he keeps. "Never again shall this cup, polluted by the lips of misfortune, be used by man." He speaks, and breaks the vessel into fragments.

'The ceremony is over; the guests with difficulty restraining their tears, take their last farewell and leave the room. One only, the nearest and dearest, is requested to remain and witness the end. Rikiu then removes his tea-gown and carefully folds it upon the mat, thereby disclosing the immaculate white death robe which it had hitherto concealed. Tenderly he gazes on the shining blade of the fatal dagger, and in exquisite verse thus addresses it:

> "Welcome to thee,
> O sword of eternity!
> Through Buddha
> And through Dharuma alike
> Thou hast cleft thy way."

With a smile upon his face Rikiu passed forth into the unknown.'

Nowhere else does one find anything approaching such ceremony but most nations have their different ideas about making tea. In Thailand they chew *miang* with salt and other condiments. (Not so different from the schoolboys' reputed food of tea-leaves on bread and butter.) In Burma they make *letpet* by pickling tea-leaves with oil and garlic, sometimes adding dried fish. Newly married couples drink from the same cup tea-leaves steeped in oil to ensure felicity till death do them part. In Kashmir they drink *cha tulch*, tea boiled with red potash, aniseed and salt. The Arabs like their tea as sweet as it can be made, and flavoured with mint. In Korea, it has been recorded, they suck raw eggs between sips of tea.

Raw eggs have quite an association with tea. A Jesuit missionary's recipe was mentioned earlier, and Richard Church in his *Over the Bridge* tells us that his father used to have an egg in his tea.

This is, of course, quite different from the Scottish 'egg to your tea', which is merely the description of a properly substantial meal. No nonsense like the English thin bread and butter and cucumber sandwiches with the crust cut off, or American cookies. Instead there are whole loaves of brown and white with butter and various jams in plenty, scones, drop-scones, currant buns, gingerbread, shortbread, cakes in variety.

Tea as a washer down of substantial meals, as well as a waker-upper, appetizer, digester and sundowner, is fully appreciated in the Dominions. The New Zealanders thrive on it. The Australians have grown into the tallest nation on it. 'Waltzing Matilda', the smoke blackened billy-can famous in song, opened up the bush. A Chinese emperor once recommended that tea water should be boiled for as long as it takes to turn crayfish red. The man who earns his living out of doors stews his tea in the billy for at least as long as it takes him to cook the rest of his meal. You get the full flavour that way, with plenty of tannin to make you leathery. In Labrador I was taught by the trappers to drop into the boiling can a match-sized piece of charred wood from the fire. It was said to reduce the 'swinged' taste.

Tea has always been an explorer's drink. It gives most for its weight. So it has been to the north end and south end of our world and also to its highest mountain – where it had to be brewed at a water boiling point well below the normal. Iced tea was the drink requested by Colonel Glenn directly he was released from his capsule after orbiting the earth, so perhaps it will be in that form that it is eventually introduced to other planets – that or with lemon in a glass.

The Eskimos delighted in tea directly they tasted it. From Greenland comes a story (I am glad to say not from my own experience so it may not be true) that to an isolated settlement in the north-west which had recently been introduced to tea there was once sent tobacco instead. The natives brewed it up and drank it, with fatal results. On the other hand, I have smoked tea, lacking tobacco. It is quite good, highly aromatic, but burns too fast.

Back to iced tea – it was the southern United States which showed the world what a good hot-weather drink it is – they and the Alpine guides, some of whom mix it with red wine to make what they claim to be the best thirst–quencher and reviver combined.

New Amsterdam made tea in the Dutch manner. A good hostess served several kinds to suit the tastes of her guests – a charming refinement. They never got milk but they were sometimes offered saffron and peach leaves for flavouring. Sugar was in 'bite and stir' boxes, lump in one partition and powdered in another. You could nibble it or put it in your tea. They knew that subtle childish pleasure of sucking something through a lump of sugar. When New Amsterdam became New York they drank tea in the English fashion. Now – the only actual difference is that it is kept in bags. But Americans are no longer on intimate terms with tea.

In Russia, as the world knows, tea is prepared with the samovar, an urn in which the liquid is kept hot by a central tube rising from the source of heat, a principle similar to that of the electric immersion heater in a boiler. The tea pot is generally kept hot on top of the samovar. The traditional method was for the hostess to quarter-fill each glass with very strong tea which was then diluted to taste with water from the samovar, and seasoned with a slice of lemon when available. As a point of interest Peter Mundy described what was evidently a samovar as being used by the Chinese during his visit to Canton Bay with Captain Weddell. In this case it was being employed for heating punch, but it seems possible that the instrument was introduced to Russia at the same time as tea.

Travelling eastward through Siberia' one is approaching the region of brick tea. It is compressed into this form while soft and damp in the early stages of its manufacture from the gum leaf. Brick tea used to be a form of currency and still represents food as well as drink, being brewed up with salt and sometimes fat and having butter and meal stirred into it. At least one great missionary journey depended on such sustenance. In 1846–8 Père Evarist Régis Huc and Père Joseph Gabet travelled from the Chinese coast to Lhasa to explore this vast region which the Roman Catholic Church hope to convert. Père Huc made notes of everything which interested him (there was little which did not) and later published his experiences in *Souvenirs d'un Voyage dans la Tartarie, le Tibet et la Chine.* Almost every incident is in some way connected with tea.

The party consisted of Père Huc, Père Gabet, their Tartar servant Samdadchienba, three camels, a black mule and a white horse. Before starting on the pilgrim road to Lhasa they collected their provisions which consisted of 'five bricks of tea, two sheeps' paunches of butter, two sacks of flour and eight sacks of *tsampa*' (barley meal). Whenever they camped, which was the general rule, they brewed tea outside their little tent, under the stars. Tartar peasants, Mongol and Tibetan herdsmen gave them tea in hospitality with the welcome, 'Drink in peace'. When occasionally they stopped at an inn they were at once offered tea. 'You must swallow oceans of tea, and that boiling hot, before they will consent to bring you anything else.' The *maître d'hôtel* was called the Governor of the Kettle. Tea was served before every meal and every meal was basically tea.

'They take a tea-cup half-filled with boiling tea; to that they add some pinches of *tsampa*, and then mix those materials into a sort of wretched paste, neither cooked nor uncooked, not hot nor cold, which is then swallowed and is considered breakfast, dinner or supper as the case may be.'

To the Frenchmen this was the worst sort of cooking but they soon learned that tea, especially when 'richly buttered', kept out the cold and sustained them on the long road.

This apprenticeship prepared them for Tibet. At the lamasery of Kounboum they attended a tea-party of 4,000 lamas.

'The pilgrim who proposes to entertain the brotherhood waits upon the superiors of the Lamasery, and, presenting to them a *khata* (ceremonial scarf), announces that he shall have the devotion to offer to the Lamas a general or special tea.

'The tea-general is for the whole Lamasery without distinction; the tea-special is given only to one of the four faculties, the selection being with the pilgrim. On the day fixed for a tea-general, after the repetition of morning prayer, the presiding Lama gives a signal for the company to retain their seats. Then forty young *Chabis*, appointed by lot, proceed to the great kitchen, and soon return laden with jars of tea; they pass along the ranks, and as they come to each Lama, the latter draws from his bosom his wooden tea-cup, and it is filled to the brim. Each drinks in silence, carefully placing a corner of his scarf before his cup, in order to modify the apparent anomaly of introducing so material a proceeding as tea-drinking into so spiritual a spot. Generally there is tea enough presented to go round twice, the tea being stronger or weaker according to the generosity of the donor. There are some pilgrims who add a slice of fresh butter for each Lama, and magnificent Amphytrions go the length, further, of oatmeal cakes. When the banquet is over, the presiding Lama solemnly proclaims the name of the pious pilgrim who has done himself the immense credit of regaling the holy family of Lamas; the pilgrim donor prostrates himself on the earth; the Lamas sing a hymn in his favour, and then march out in procession past their prostrate benefactor, who does not rise until the last of the Lamas has disappeared.

'Offerings of this sort are very little for each individual Lama; but when you reflect that on such occasions there are assembled together more than 4,000 tea-drinkers, you may easily estimate that the aggregate expense becomes a very serious affair. In the Lamasery at Kounboum, one single tea-general, without either butter or cakes, costs fifty ounces of silver, or about twenty pounds.'

For the Tibetan, butter is as necessary an addition to tea as milk with us. At the same lamasery the Frenchmen saw the Festival of the Flowers. 'The Flowers . . . consist of representations, profane and religious, in which all the Asiatic nations are introduced with their peculiar physiognomies and their distinguishing costumes. Persons, places, apparel, decorations – all are formed of fresh butter.'

The preparations for this festival lasted for three months during which twenty lamas selected for their artistic skill worked with their hands in cold water lest the warmth of their fingers should mar the images which they created. Thousands of images of 'exquisite finish', dozens of complete tableaux were created. But the show lasted for only a single night. Then all these works of art were destroyed by the artists themselves.

Once in Tibet the Frenchmen were given tea from a silver pot, in a cup of jade with a golden saucer on a lacquered table. This was an elegance which they scarcely felt themselves worthy to enjoy. They had bought their furlined clothes second-hand and never changed them. A man cannot detect, only suspect, his own odour, but somehow they had kept a nose for others. Père Huc, evidently a connoisseur, evokes the picture of a wine-taster choosing between two vintages when he tries to analyse the difference between the smells of Chinese and Tartars in their airless huts. He decides that the Tartar bouquet is stronger but the Chinese more sickening.

After two years they returned to Macao and tea to which only boiling water had been added. Even long custom had not reconciled them to the coarse Tartar tea-brick and its greasy adjuncts. Père Huc admits, 'We drank it in default of something better.'

II

The right way to make tea is how you like it. But certain data may help you to decide the wisdom of your choice.

First the water. If it is not pure and fresh it will impart a flavour to the tea. As to temperature and time of boiling, Gervas Huxley, Vice-chairman of the Tea Market Expansion Board, describes in *Talking of Tea* an experiment which is as instructive as it is simple. Put an equal measure of tea into three tumblers. Fill the first with water which has not quite reached the boil, the second with water which has just come vigorously to the boil, and the third with water which has been boiling for ten minutes. After five minutes – the standard period for infusion – it will be found that about half the leaves in the first glass have risen to the surface and remained there. In the second, after travelling individually up and down in a lively manner they have all settled. In the third they will have formed a close-knit soggy ball at the bottom and scarcely moved at all.

The reason is that water below boiling point does not extract all the ingredients from the leaves. Water which has just reached the boil is still full of air particles which help to distribute the leaves so that the water has the maximum effect on each, an action which does not take place with the flat and airless water used in the third tumbler. From this one sees that just boiling water has the maximum effect.

Before deciding how long tea should be left standing it is necessary to know something of its chemistry. Its two most important constituents are caffein and polyphenols. The finer the tea – that is to say the finer the leaves from which it is made – the more of these constituents are present in it.

The immediate comfort which a cup of tea gives is due to its warmth. This is a purely physical stimulus. Some minutes elapse before the caffein makes itself felt. Caffein is a drug which acts on the central nervous system, on the muscles including the heart muscles, and on the kidneys. Its most noticeable effect in moderate doses is to produce a condition of wakefulness and increased mental activity. It also increases the efficiency of the muscles and stimulates respiration. We need not bother about immoderate doses for it would be very difficult to swallow them in the form of tea. A nine-pounds-a-year drinker, which is the average in Great Britain, swallows about four-and-a-half grains of caffein a day which is below a medicinal dose, let alone a harmful quantity.

The polyphenols are what ordinary people call tannin. It gives the strength to tea – much of the taste, in fact, as opposed to the aroma. It has been argued by critics of tea that tannin constipates. But you would have to drink a frightening amount of strong black tea before you noticed that effect. When milk is added the casein in it allays the tannin – in other words it softens the taste. The only final effect is that protein is added. Thus, though a cup of black tea contains only about four calories, a spoonful of milk adds ten calories to this and a lump of sugar, which has no chemical effect, a further twenty-five. Since an active man needs 2,500 to 3,000 calories a day, tea cannot be considered as a food. Nor does it claim to be a useful supplier of vitamins.

The longer the tea is left infusing the more caffein and tannin (polyphenols) are extracted from the leaves, and therefore consumed by the drinker.

Mr C. R. Harler in *The Culture and Marketing of Tea* provides a table which shows the proportion of these and of the soluble solids which are extracted first by a five-minutes' infusion which is later watered, and then by a thirty-three minutes' infusion.

Infusion	*Caffein*	*Poly-phenols*	*Soluble Solids*
	%	%	%
1. 5 minutes under cosy	80	40	60
Second brew, 20 minutes under cosy	20	20	25
2. 33 minutes under cosy	100	60	85

The second, long brew extracts as much as the other two together.

Tea kept hot in a thermos, not on the leaves, undoubtedly goes off in quality after a few hours. The chemical explanation of this is obscure, but the fact obvious.

It is simplest to stick to the housewife's simple rule – warm the pot, put in one teaspoon of tea for each person and one for the pot, pour in freshly drawn, just boiling water and let it stand for five minutes. But vary it as you will, for a little of what you fancy does you good.

CHAPTER VIII

Sixteen Thousand Miles by the Log

Their canvas flared across the China Sea,
Back in the misty 'forties ere the steam
And plate steel from the Tyne swept every lea,
Crowding the sail to yards where they might dream
Of vanished greatness when the seas would cream
Across their surging prows or washing lanes;
And o'er the waste to catch Nantucket's gleam –
Canton to Boston with the golden gains.

Thomas J. Murray

THE story of tea for the Western world is also that of ships and seamen. We began with Weddell's small, unhandy fleet. Those of his ships which covered the whole distance spent two years and eight months on the round trip and, according to Peter Mundy, sailed 36,204 miles. Then comes the long calm of the East India Company's massive monopoly which ended in 1833. The next significant date is 1849 when Britain's Navigation Laws designed to prevent foreign ships from bringing tea to England were virtually repealed – which meant free trade and competition. The end of the era was 1869 when the Suez Canal was opened.

It will be noticed that the birth of steam has not been mentioned. For one thing its effective emergence cannot be precisely dated. For another, the tea-clippers which in the latter half of the nineteenth century had reached the peak of scientific evolution maintained their superiority over steamers in both speed and cheapness while the only route was round the Cape of Good Hope. It was the Canal which gave the steamers an invincible superiority.

During the first few decades after trade with China became possible the East India Company used chartered vessels generally of less than 500 tons and indifferent seaworthiness. Sailors ready to undertake a dangerous and exceedingly uncomfortable voyage of two years or more were rough illiterate men. For that reason the diary of a man before the mast at that period is of exceptional interest. A unique example is the journal of Edward Barlow which covers the end of the seventeenth and the beginning of the eighteenth century. This consists of some 225,000 words of neat manuscript, and I have worked from the transcription made by Basil Lubbock and published by Hurst and Blackett.

Barlow came of a poor family and taught himself to write. He sailed to both the West and East Indies and made four voyages to China, the last in 1702 when he was sixty-one years old. He rose to the rank of chief mate. How for so many years he managed to keep so beautifully written a diary, and to illustrate it with hundreds of striking drawings is a mystery. A smelly and crowded forecastle without a chair let alone a table and a crude oil lamp as the only light is as bad a workroom as one can well imagine.

Ships at the start of a long voyage were invariably overcrowded with men and stores. 'We left two of our guns at home,' he wrote in 1701, 'carrying no more than twenty pieces of ordnance in our ship, for she was very full and pestered with passengers and their goods.'

Bad weather played havoc with a crowded ship. 'Many times we could not carry enough sail, driving to and fro and doing much damage and loss in our fresh provisions, having drowned a hundred fowls, hens, cocks, turkeys and geese, and several pigs and hogs and some sheep, and bruising much the live bullocks we had on board.'

He described crossing the equator: 'In the beginning of May we crossed the Equinoctial Line, every man who had not been there before paying his bottle of strong waters as a forfeit, it being merily drank out by all the rest who had been there before, an old custom among seamen.'

By the hit-or-miss navigation of that time they crossed the Indian Ocean, running west until they were among seaweed, and then turned north for Java Head.

Sickness was rife among the crew: 'If a man be not very moderate or careful it is a thousand to one if he catch not some disease or another presently, the bloody flukes being the rifest which is seldom helped and killeth a lusty strong man in ten days.'

He himself suffered from the 'bloody flukes'. He describes the lot of the sick seamen in the forecastle:

'We having no other thing to eat and drink and restore our health and comfort ourselves with, unless we eat a piece of hard biscuit cake, or a piece of old salt beef or pork, and maybe both stinking and rotten, having lain in pickle one year or two, and nothing to drink but a little fresh water, many times both stinking and dirty, and yet cannot get half enough of.'

He gives a bad character to ships' doctors who would go and see a sick man –

and take him by the hand when they hear he has been sick two or three days, thinking that is soon enough, and feeling his pulse when he is half dead, asking him when he was at stool and how he feels himself and how he has slept, and then giving him some of their medicine upon the point of a knife which doeth as much good to him as a blow upon the pate with a stick.'

The next attention the man received might be to 'sew him up in an old blanket or piece of canvas and tie to his feet two or three cannon bullets and so heave him overboard'.

Sea fights with national enemies or privateers were common. A larger ship would take and loot a smaller one almost as a matter of course. Barlow was made prisoner by the Dutch, but released.

Only once did he visit Whampoa, on the other occasions anchoring off Macao or the Ladrones Islands. He had a poor opinion of the Chinese – who reciprocated the sentiments of the common sailors. He gives a quaint description:

'Their men keep themselves very little beards, it being their use to pluck out the hairs as they grow yet never shave them with a razor, their beards growing thin and straggling like Salisbury Plain, here a bush and there a thief, whereof ariseth the old saying of a Chinaman having but nine hairs in his beard.'

Back in England between voyages he confesses to a romance:

'Falling into the company of one of our neighbour's daughters I took a great fancy to be in her company as often as I could, and she was the first that ever I professed any kind of real love for, and I did gain her affection so far that we did in part or wholly promise one another to keep our love entire till my arrival off my next voyage which I did intend to make to the East Indies, and then at my coming back into the country again to unite ourselves in wed-lock.

'Yet I could not fix and ground my love so far upon her that I could keep myself from professing the same to some others.'

As first mate Barlow received £6 10s a month, 'pretty good wages'. But he despaired of ever growing rich: 'Now to be grown near to sixty years of age I could not well expect much good fortune to be before me after finding little in so many years before; but to hope for true happiness in the world to come is the best and lastingest good we can hope for.' Poor disillusioned, tired old sailorman!

As an indication of the sort of goods first exported from China, a list of Barlow's last cargo is of interest.

'On the first day of February 1702 we set sail from a place called Whampow in the river of Canton in China, praying to God for a good passage to England, being a full ship and laden with goods, namely:

'200 chests of China and Japan ware, porcelain, and 507 chests of copper; 122 chests of Quicksilver, 416 tubs and baskets of sugar candy; 155 bags of Nox Vomacka, 43 bags of Galingall; 28 bags of Gourege; 28 chests of rubarbe; 14 Scrivitoris, small; 13 chests of lacquered ware; 23 chests of China Lack; 481 balls or bundles of raw silk; two chests of fans; two tubs of oil for lacquering; one chest of turtle shell; 4 chests of vermilion; 83 chests of tea; 60 large jars of green ginger; 4822 pieces of China wrought silk of several sorts; 70 chests of screens; and a great deal of loose China and Japan ware which we packed upon board.'

Later, when the East India Company had become rich and well established in both India and China, its ships were in the eyes of the period things of wonder and admiration. The significance of the Company's monopoly, combined with the Navigation Laws, must once more be stressed. Under the monopoly no British firms were permitted to compete with John Company in the East, and by the Navigation Laws no foreign merchant ships could enter a British port except with produce from its own country. Where tea was concerned the only possible rival would have been a Chinese junk. So provided the tea did not deteriorate too much before reaching London it did not matter how long it took upon the voyage. Thus the speed of the Company's vessels was of minor importance. Before it came security, carrying capacity, and the comfort of the passengers – often people of importance. Other sailors called the East Indiamen tea-wagons, but that was not quite just.

They were armed like warships. They fought their battles in the early days and their record is a fine one. They were wide of beam to provide the maximum capacity for cargo. They were blunt of bow because that was the age-old fashion. As for comfort, everyone on board was well looked after. The common sailors had plenty of good food and quite as much rum and other forms of alcohol as was good for them. The officers lived in a style worthy of their rank. The passengers were fed and quartered luxuriously, yet personal comfort depended even more than it does today on possessing a good sailor for a stomach, for those kettle-bottomed queens of the sea must have rolled in everything except a dead calm.

Seduced by the sleek loveliness and exciting achievements of the clippers which followed it is easy to be patronizing about the East Indiamen. But in fact they were unique. In fighting power and official backing they were almost the Royal Navy. They were smart as the ships of the Navy. They were authorized to fly its long coach-whip pennant.

Dr Dowding described a ship which must have been sold to a private company at the termination of the East India Company's period in China.

'The double-decker is seen with her tall slender masts towering above the others (at Whampoa), and with her yards squared and delicate rigging extended with the minutest nicety; the well-bleached awning above the deck stretched with the greatest care; the gilded figure-head and ornamental stern, and the sides fresh painted and shining with varnish. As she lies thus moored in the middle of the stream, and with her little pinnace just seen beyond her anchored near the shore, she only requires a few guns peeping out of her open ports to complete the picture and transform her into a man-of-war, and one of the finest in the British navy. Borne lightly on the water, her tall spars are reflected towards you, and her double side checkered with black and white is portraid in the water immediately beneath, resembling the squares on a chess board made of ivory and ebony.'

You notice the comparison with a naval vessel. Both the men-of-war and the East Indiamen were made of timber seasoned in salt water until it was almost as hard as iron, held together with through-and-through copper bolts. They were made to stand up to both storms and gunfire by sheer strength. But this one, probably unladen at the time, looked light to Dr Dowding who had never seen a clipper. Taste in beauty is as conservative as taste in food. To him, and to all at that time – certainly all who were British – the East Indiamen looked just right.

Dowding was struck by the fresh paint and decoration. In the days of John Company the officers and crew matched their ships for elegance. The Captain's uniform was a blue coat with black velvet lapels, cuffs and collar, with gold embroidery and gilt buttons carrying the Company's crest. His waistcoat and breeches were deep buff. His stock was black. He wore side arms. His officers were scarcely less magnificent, and his sailors were well turned out. They kept the ship to perfection. They had to. So long as they behaved themselves they were looked after for the rest of their lives. After eight years of good service a man was entitled to a pension. If he was killed or maimed on duty his dependants were cared for. But no slackness of any sort was permitted.

The officers on inspection duty wore white gloves, and if these were soiled by touching the brasswork there was painful trouble for the man responsible. All faults of discipline were severely dealt with. Virtue, and seniority, were rewarded. It was as simple and old-fashioned as that.

Religious observance was compulsory, the Captain being commanded by his superiors on land 'to keep up the worship of Almighty God, under a penalty of two guineas for every omission not satisfactorily accounted for in the log-book'.

The Captains were well rewarded, as in proportion was all

the ship's company. He could make £6,000–£10,000 a year from his pay and 'indulgencies', which latter included 56½ tons of cargo space and a part of the dunnage. The *Oxford Dictionary* definition of dunnage is 'stuff stowed over, under and among the cargo goods to prevent moisture and chafing'. This could and did include much valuable merchandise. Junior officers got their share of this benefit. With good pay and sufficient social prestige the Company's maritime service attracted a valuable and neglected section of society, the younger sons of good families. The East Indiamen were well officered, much better manned throughout than was the rest of the merchant service.

The life was not exacting, for hard work only starts on a sailing ship when you try to go fast with a minimum crew. The officers kept three watches, four hours on and eight off. The ample crew kept two. They slept in the between-decks in hammocks which were stowed in nettings when the boatswain's pipe sounded at seven bells. The decks were scrubbed and holystoned, and then all hands had breakfast. Twice a week the between-decks were also thoroughly cleaned. There followed gun drill, cutlass and musket drill, courts martial and punishments with the cat-o'-nine tails. In the dog watches the crew got their ration of grog and were encouraged to sky-lark. On Saturdays the drink ration was increased and the toast was 'Sweethearts and Wives'. There was music and dancing. In the evenings, if there was any sign of bad weather blowing up, sail was shortened, the ship snugged down for the night.

Such was the tradition which scarcely changed in more than 200 years, any more than the ships did in design. This dignified service ended with the monopoly. The Company knew it could not compete with private enterprise. The ships were sold. It is proof of the excellent material put into them that even those disposed of for breaking up fetched about £7,000.

The private shipping companies managed fairly well while the Navigation Laws remained in force. They were still free from the competition of foreign vessels. The real test started with the beginning of free trade.

There is doubt and argument as to when the first clipper was launched. But on 3 December 1850 the first American clipper entered a British port. The *Oriental* moored in the

West India Docks ninety-seven days after leaving Hong Kong with a cargo of 1,600 tons of tea. She had set out *against* the north-west monsoon and beaten the British ships hollow on their own run. There she lay in the Thames, tall, slim and beautiful, as different in appearance from the sturdy British vessels as is a greyhound from a bulldog. From the tops of her tall raking masts to the waterline she was as sleek and neat as if she had just been fitted out, although directly prior to her record-breaking westward run she had sailed from New York to China in eighty-one days. (No snugging down at night here, nor lack of maintenance while at sea!) In China she had at once picked up her cargo at a freight charge of £6 per ton while British ships were canvassing for cargoes at £3 10s a ton . . . There was much for the crowds of English visitors to discuss, with alarm as well as admiration.

The Times came out with a leading article:

'The rapid increase of population in the United States, augmented by an annual immigration of nearly three hundred thousand from these isles, is a fact that forces itself on the notice and interest of the most unobservant and uncurious. All these promise to develop the resources of the United States to such an extent as to compel us to a competition as difficult as it is unavoidable. We must run a race with our gigantic and unshackled rival. We must set our long-practised skill, our steady industry, and our dogged determination, against his youth, ingenuity, and ardor. It is a father who runs a race with his son. A fell necessity constrains us and we must not be beat. Let our ship-builders and employers take warning in time. There will always be an abundant supply of vessels, good enough and fast enough for short voyages. The coal-trade can take care of itself, for it will always be a refuge for the destitute. But we want fast vessels for the long voyages, which otherwise will fall into American hands. It is fortunate that the Navigation Laws have been repealed in time to destroy these false and unreasonable expectations, which might have lulled the ardor of British competition. We now all start together with a fair field and no favour. The American captain can call at London, and the British captain can pursue his voyage to New York. Who can complain? Not we. We trust that our countrymen will not be beaten; but if they should be, we shall know that they deserve it.'

The Times was being courageous but rather more pessimistic than it need have been. In 1839 a schooner-rigged 'clipper', the *Scottish Maid*, had been launched at Aberdeen for use in home waters. She had been followed by others which, amply manned and strongly armed, had proved their value in running opium on the coast of China. They did so well that the Americans copied them. But they were small, 100–200 tons, racing yachts rather than merchantmen. Therefore they were not strictly clippers in the later meaning of the word.

A clipper is a *large* vessel designed to go fast. The British knew how to build for speed. All maritime nations did, if they had eyes to see. The Arab dhow a thousand years before had evolved into the almost perfect shape for sailing fast. In Britain the races between revenue cutters and smuggling craft had done a lot to increase speed. So had America's experiences in her wars. What nobody had done, and what the Americans were first to do, was to build large cargo-carrying vessels, 400–1,000 tons or more, with the lines of these small, fast craft. When this came about, the term 'clipper' was restricted to these vessels alone. The word probably derives from the slang 'clip' meaning fast, which schoolboys still use – 'go at a good clip' – and with which Dryden described his falcon which 'clips it down the wind'.

This, briefly, is the story of the clipper's evolution. Donald McKay, an American of Scottish extraction, began building ships which were considerably longer in proportion to their

(a)

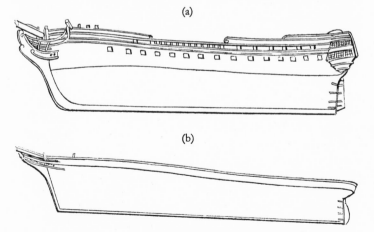

(b)

Typical lines of (a) an East Indiaman and (b) a clipper

beam than had been the fashion before. Being thus slimmer they were faster. Speed had been something of a danger until then because the foremast, placed where tradition demanded, close to the bow, tended to push the bow down before a strong wind. McKay moved the foremast farther aft. His sharp vessels proved their worth on trans-Atlantic passenger runs.

But bows remained full. Their cross-section was similar to that of an inverted bell. Above the waterline they looked as tradition said they should – and indeed they were handsome. They were also practical at moderate speeds for as they rose and fell their wide flare smacked the spray outwards so that little water fell upon deck. But at high speeds this continuous and violent pounding was damaging to the structure of the ship.

The Aberdeen firm of Alexander Hall overcame this in the '40s by increasing the forward rake of the bow – in unnautical terms by making the bow overhang run – backwards at a vertical angle from top to bottom. Thus the bow-lines above the water level could be finer, with less flare, and they therefore scissored into the waves instead of pounding through them. So there was much less jarring of the ship's structure. But sometimes the bows scissored down too easily and too far, and anyone working in the bows was liable to be washed away.

It is at once evident that there were dangers in sharpening the ship. She became a more delicate instrument. But this was atched bmy the increasing skill of captain and crew. The whole art of sailing was rapidly improving.

A final word about the clipper's bow. It could be sharp as a knife. But the forefoot – where bow meets keel – could not be too gentle a curve or the ship failed to grip the sea when sailing into the wind. The bow of the *Cutty Sark* – a great clipper unfortunately born too late, in the year when the Suez Canal was opened – carried these principles to the logical extreme. Her transverse bow section was a sharp V, her forefoot a true angle as opposed to a curve.

A slim stern, although it further increased speed, also had its dangers. It might cut down through a following wave too deeply instead of being raised by it. So the risk of being pooped – of the stern being buried by a wave – increased. But this was accepted, and overcome by skilful seamanship.

The other most striking features of the fully developed

clipper were the backward raking masts and their increased height, and the decks cleared of clutter which might hinder fast sailing. They looked swift creatures, and they were. At last a vessel had been evolved which could do what had seemed impossible before – get quickly enough from China to America or England to avoid the necessity of putting in anywhere *en route* for stores and water.

The swift and lovely *Oriental* in the West India Docks shook some of the Victorian smugness out of the British public. She shook the journalists. She shook the Admiralty, which asked permission to take off her lines. But the British merchant captains had seen American clippers before – in Chinese waters when British ports were still denied to them by the Navigation Acts, or perhaps in mid-ocean when one had gone creaming past them through still water while they lay virtually becalmed. They had seen, had been impressed and taken action when they got home.

The *Stornoway*, a clipper of 506 tons was launched in Aberdeen at the end of that same year, 1850. She was soon followed by the *Chrysolite* and others. The race was on – 'a fair field and no favours'. It was an exclusively British and American race: there were no other nations in it at any time. The first of the season's tea to reach market won the best prices so there was an automatic prize quite apart from betting and bonuses. The tea-clippers ran the greatest races there have ever been, or are likely to be, rivalling the Derby for excitement and popular interest and lasting about a hundred days. It is a great pity that the Civil War forced the Americans to withdraw at the height of the competition.

At the start, too, the British were granted a certain amount of grace, with the opportunity of making up for lost time, because the beginning of free trade almost coincided with the gold rush to California. There was a heavy demand for fast ships to carry the hopeful from New York, round Cape Horn and up the Pacific coast. But these clippers, so long as their crews did not desert for the gold fields, often returned by crossing the Pacific in ballast, picking up a cargo of tea in China and racing it to London or New York.

The ships were not everything, of course. Designs can be copied. Whether they were a success or failure rested with the officers and crew who had not only to force their vessel to the limit, and keep her at that pitch for three months or more – a sufficient strain in itself – but also maintain spars and rigging in racing trim. What sort of men were these?

The English merchant sailors had the tradition of Trafalgar behind them – the gay and reckless men who drank gunpowder with their rum before battle. They had grown into a race quite different from landsmen, thinking differently, speaking almost a different language for those ships with their miles of cordage, forest of spars, acres of canvas, demanded a vocabulary almost as large as they could muster. They were experts at their craft, but simple souls. To them the land was a place to get drunk and make love on. The sea was their profession. They were warm-hearted, impulsive, superstitious, brave, unruly. Of course they were not fundamentally different from other men but their natural qualities were accentuated by a life which seemed to prevent them from growing up as far as responsibility was concerned. They were constricted like boys at school, with no feminine influence – except the ship. Their days and nights were governed by certain rules which, being concerned only with the efficient running of the ship, had no moral basis. If they transgressed them they were punished, and as a point of honour took their dozen or two lashes on the bare back without a murmur – and without repentance. Their masters were by no means always models of morality and sobriety. But in the better ships at least both officers and men loved their vessel with a fanatical loyalty. You might more safely insult a sailor's woman than his ship. In the race of 1866 one clipper crew to a man backed their ship with a month's pay to beat their chief rival.

In American ships there was as a rule only a small proportion of American-born sailors. Young Americans went to sea with the firm intention of becoming officers quickly, and they either succeeded or gave up the sea. Few indeed, at least in clippers, served their whole working lives before the mast. Thus the clipper crews were as mixed in nationality as is, by origin, the population of the United States today.

There were generally some British in the forecastle, for the Americans offered better pay which tempted many, particularly the best seamen who felt themselves insufficiently rewarded. They knew every aspect of their work. The Liverpool Irish, on the other hand, had the reputation of being tough to the extent of being almost unrulable, fearless aloft in any weather but limited in skill. Fighting the elements in a gale they were at their best. Unfortunately they were also at their best fighting their fellow sailors or the officers. They were partial to a mutiny. It was as well not to have too many of them in a crew. In any case they were no use at all at the many tasks of maintenance. (Chafe was the enemy which had to be fought throughout the voyage by splicings and replacements.) There were Italians and Russians, Frenchmen and Africans, Portuguese, Chinamen and Spaniards (of varying character and capacity). There were others – often too many – who were only recognizable as the stuff with which prisons are filled. These were a curse to any captain. The best all-rounders were the Scandinavians – clean, hard-working, obedient, excellent sailors both aloft and with marline-spike and sailmaker's needle.

This was the age when the chanty came into its own. These songs originated – partly at least: there were some earlier sources – early in the nineteenth century with white, half-white and negro stevedores at Mobile and New Orleans who sang them while loading bales of cotton. The sailors copied them, sometimes amending the wild words half meaningless to landsmen, giving them something of the surge and roar of the sea which polite modern choirs can never copy. They were of practical value for rousing the spirit and giving the rhythm of effort at capstan or hawser. A good chanty leader was worth four men in a watch.

It was to hear these songs as the anchor was got in that crowds gathered in the London Docks or Battery Park when a clipper was putting to sea – for that and to see how the mate would manage his crew who traditionally rolled aboard full as barrels with liquor. On American ships there was nothing stronger than coffee, but the crews made up for this ashore.

Arthur H. Clark, a sailing-ship captain himself, gave in *The Clipper Ship Era* the best account there is of a clipper putting to sea. It would be a shame to paraphrase it so I shall give it in full.

'This is an anxious day for the mate, for, while he receives his instructions from the Captain in a general way, yet every detail of getting the ship to sea is in his hands; and though he seems careless and unconcerned, his nerves are on edge and every sense alert; his eyes are all over the ship. He is sizing up each man in his crew and getting his gauge; when he strikes a chord of sympathy, he strikes hard, and when his keen instinct detects a note of discord, he strikes still harder, lifting his men along with a curse here, a joke there, and ever tightening his firm but not unkindly grasp of authority. The mate is not hunting for trouble – all that he wants is for his men to do their work and show him enough respect so that it will not become his un-pleasant duty to hammer them into shape. He knows that this is his day, and that it is the decisive day of the voyage, for before the ship passes out by Sandy Hook his moral victory will be lost or won, with no appeal to Admiralty Boards or Courts of Justice. He knows, too, that a score of other mates and their captains are looking on with keen interest to see how he handles his crew, and their opinion is of far greater value to him than the decrees of Senates; so he intends to lay himself out and give them something worth looking at.

'There is a crisp north-easterly breeze, and the blue waters of the bay dance and frolic in the sweet June sunshine. The crew are all on board, with the Captain and pilot in consultation on the quarterdeck; it is nearly high water, and the tide will soon run ebb. The mate takes charge of the topgallant forecastle, with the third mate and the boatswain to assist him, while, the second mate, with the fourth mate and boatswain's mate work the main deck and stand by to look after the chain as it comes in over the windlass.

'As the crew muster on the forecastle they appear to be a motley gang, most British and Scandinavian, with a sprinkling of Spaniards, Portuguese and Italians, and one or two Americans. Some wear thick, coarse, red, blue, or gray flannel shirts, others blue dungaree jumpers, or cotton shirts of various colors; their trousers are in a variety of drabs, blues, grays, and browns, supported by leather belts or braces; they wear stiff or soft felt hats or woollen caps of many colors. But no clothes that were ever invented could disguise these men; their bronzed, weather-beaten faces and sun-baked, tattooed arms, with every swing of their bodies, betray them as sailormen, and good ones too, above the average even in those days. They would no more submit to being put into uniforms or to the cut-and-dried discipline of a man-of-war, than they would think of eating their food at a table with knives and forks.

'They are all pretty full of alcohol, but the sailor instinct is so strong in them that they do their work as well, some of them perhaps better, than if they were sober. There is no romance about them or about any part of their lives; they are simply common, every-day sailors, and will never be anything else, unless they happen to encounter some inspired writer of fiction; then it is difficult to say what may become of them. Some of them have much good in their natures, others are saturated with evil, and all need to be handled with tact and judgment, for too much severity, or on the other hand any want of firmness, may lead to trouble, which means the free use of knives, belaying pins, and knuckle-dusters.

'Now the flood-tide begins to slacken, and as the ship swings to the wind, the order is passed along from aft to man the windlass and heave short. We hear the mate sing out in a pleasant, cheery voice: "Now, then, boys, heave away on the windlass breaks; strike a light, it's duller than an old graveyard." And the chantyman, in an advanced stage of hilarious intoxication, gay as a skylark, sails into song:

> '"In eighteen hundred and forty-six,
> I found myself in the hell of a fix,
> A-working on the railway, the railway, the railway.
> Oh, poor Paddy works on the railway.

> '"In eighteen hundred and forty-seven,
> When Dan O'Connolly went to heaven,
> He worked upon the railway, the railway, the railway.
> Poor Paddy works on the railway, the railway.

> '"In eighteen hundred and forty-eight,
> I found myself bound for the Golden Gate,
> A-working on the railway, the railway.
> Oh, poor Paddy works on the railway, the railway.

> '"In eighteen hundred and forty-nine,
> I passed my time in the Black Ball Line,
> A-working on the railway, the railway,
> I weary on the railway,
> Poor Paddy works on the railway, the railway."

'And so on to the end of the century, or till the mate sings out, "Vast heaving", lifts his hand, and reports to the Captain: "The anchor's apeak, sir." "Very good, sir, loose sails fore and aft." "Aye, aye, sir." "Aloft there some of you and loose sails. One hand stop in the tops and cross-trees to overhaul the gear." "Aye, aye, sir. Royals and skysails?" "Yes, royals and skysails; leave the staysails fast." "Lay out there, four or five of you, and loose the head sails." "Here, you fellow in the green-spotted shirt, lay down out of that; there's men enough up there now to eat those sails." "Mr. Sampson, take some of your men aft and look after the main and mizzen; put a hand at the wheel; as he goes along let him clear the ensign halliards; while you're waiting lay that accommodation ladder in on deck; leave the spanker fast." "On the foretopsail yard, there, if you cut that gasket, I'll split your damned skull; cast it adrift, you lubber." "Boatswain, get your watch tackles along to the topsail sheets." "Aye, aye, sir." "Here, some of you gentlemen's sons in disguise, get that fishdavit out; hook on the pendant; overhaul the tackle down ready for hooking on." "Mainskysail yard there, don't make those gaskets up, my boy; fetch them in along the yard, and make fast to the tye."

'By this time the sails are loose and the gaskets made up; courses, topsails, topgallantsails royals, and skysails flutter in their gear, and the clipper feels the breath of life. "Sheet home the topsails." "Aye, aye, sir." "Boatswain, look out for those clew-lines at the main; ease down handsomely as the sheets come home." "Foretop there, overhaul your buntlines, look alive!" "Belay your port maintopsail sheet; clap a watch tackle on the starboard sheet and rouse her home." "Maintop there, lay down on the main-yard and light the foot of that sail over the stay." "That's well, belay starboard." "Well the mizzentopsail sheets, belay." "Now then, my bullies, lead out your topsail halliards fore and aft and masthead her." "Aye, aye, sir." By this time the mate has put some ginger into the crew and longshoremen, and they walk away with the three topsail halliards:

> '"Away, way, way, yar.
> We'll kill Paddy Doyle for his boots."

'"Now then, long pulls, my sons." "Here, you chantyman, haul off your boots, jump on that maindeck capstan and strike a light; the best in your locker." "Aye, aye, sir." And the three topsail-yards go aloft with a ringing chanty that can be heard up in Beaver Street:

> '"Then up aloft that yard must go,
> Whiskey for my Johnny.
> Oh, whiskey is the life of man,
> Whiskey, Johnny.

I thought I heard the old man say,
Whiskey, for my Johnny.
We are bound away this very day,
Whiskey, Johnny.
A dollar a day is a white man's pay,
Whiskey for my Johnny.
Oh, whiskey killed my sister Sue,
Whiskey, Johnny,
And whiskey killed the old man, too,
Whiskey for my Johnny.
Whiskey's gone, what shall I do?
Whiskey Johnny,
Oh, whiskey's gone, and I'll go too,
Whiskey for my Johnny."

'"Belay your maintopsail halliards." "Aye, aye, sir." And so
the canvas is set fore and aft, topsails, topgallantsails, royals, and
skysails, flat as boards, the inner and outer jibs are run up and
the sheets hauled to windward; the main- and after-yards are
braced sharp to the wind, the foretopsail is laid to the mast, and
the clipper looks like some great seabird ready for flight. The
anchor is hove up to:

'"I wish I was in Slewer's Hall,
Lowlands, lowlands, hurra, my boys,
A-drinking luck to the old Black Ball,
My dollar and a half a day."

'And while some of the hands bring the anchor to the rail
with cat and fish tackle, and:

'"A Yankee sloop came down the river,
Hah, hah, rolling John,
Oh, what do you think that sloop had in her?
Hah, hah, rolling John,
Monkey's hide and bullock's liver,
Hah, hah, rolling John,"

the rest of the crew fill away the foreyard, draw away the head
sheets, and check in the after yards. As the ship pays off, and
gathers way in the slack water, the longshoremen and runners
tumble over the side into the Whitehall boats, the crowd at
Battery Park gives three parting cheers, the ensign is dipped,
and the clipper is on her way.'

There was little difference in the sailing time to China from New York or London. The quickest route was by no means necessarily the shortest. The British often swung wide into the Atlantic. On the outward voyage the ships of both nations went far south of the Cape of Good Hope until they reached the Roaring Forties which hustled them eastward across the southern end of the Indian Ocean. Then they turned northeast to find their way by one of several possible channels through the East Indies to the China Sea. In these days of shipping lanes narrow almost as roads, it is hard to realize how widely varied were the sailing routes. Much depended on a master's skill, courage and enterprise before precise charts of rocks, winds and currents were available.

The outward passage was not pressed as hard as the homeward, for cargoes were generally small and there was no premium for arriving first. Still, it was an advantage to arrive early and essential to arrive before the season's teas reached the port. The master of the *Chrysolite* described this incident on the clipper's maiden voyage:

'In the Indian Ocean we had a gale from the west, and the tremendous seas that incessantly swept over the stern caused great injury to some of my men. My chief officer had his skull severely hurt. I did my best to plaster and bandage the wound, but had scarcely done it before I was called to attend to one of the men who had his thigh broken. We shortened sail and lay-to for a while, and I set the limb as well as I could.

'Altogether six of the men were severely injured by the heavy sea, and I know not how I escaped as all through that dark night I stood watching the steering. At daylight we sighted St Paul's Island, and now saw that our misfortunes, by stopping the ship, had probably been the means of saving our lives. Had we not laid-to at the time we did, we should have been thrown on the island, and in that dark night and furious sea not one of us could have escaped.'

There were other dangers besides gales and rocks. In 1862 the *Lord of the Isles* caught fire at sea from spontaneous combustion. The ship's company managed to reach Macao in open boats, but only after having been twice boarded by pirates.

The homeward races did not start with a starting-gun. The first ship to find a cargo and load it was the first off. So the days in port, once bargaining for the tea was over, were as hectic as those at sea. But let us first look back at the more leisurely period before free trade and keen competition. There have always been the good old days.

Dr Dowding again:

'When the first chop of tea arrives alongside a ship the joyful event is announced by the cheers of the sailors. Then the process of loading commences. Down come the clerks and linguists as before. There is a domestic, a clerk, a police-runner from the Hoppo, a court-going-man, and an accountant and interpreter from the ship's linguist. These men spread out their tables and tea pots on the poop as before and take tally of the cargo as it is brought on board. The chops (lighters) are then unloaded, those which contain black teas consisting of about six hundred chests, while those which bring down the green kind contain from fifty to five hundred. They are then passed down the hatchways and successively stowed away; the crevices between them being filled up with small articles. The dunnage usually brought at the present time to England consists chiefly of cassia, or that species of bamboo called partridge canes which are used in this country for umbrellas. . . .

'The cargo is now complete, with the exception of that which is perhaps to be taken in at Lintin, and preparations are therefore made for leaving the river. The top and topgallant masts are again hoisted, the yards squared and the running rigging. [In those days ships waited so long for their cargoes that they un-rigged while lying at Whampoa.] The sails are bent, the top-sails let free, and finally the ship is unmoored. The decks are crowded at this time with native tradesmen and wash girls who are busily employed in settling their accounts with the foreigners. The Compradore and his men are also on board, providing the stores required for the voyage.

'Olo Ackow himself comes on the last day and brings with him the parting presents. Every man in the ship receives a *cum-shaw* according to his rank. These offerings usually consist of large baskets of oranges and pots of sweetmeats, and are supplied in such abundance that it is difficult to know where to stow them on account of the close quarters assigned to each person during the homeward passage. It may readily be supposed that these presents are given and received with the kindliest feelings, so that when the capstan bars are manned and the anchor raised to the music of the seamen's song, hearty good wishes are exchanged between many of the natives and the Fan-quis.

'A kindly shake of the hand and the words, "I chin-chin you wery fine voyage" accompany the old man over the side of the vessel into the boat. As the ship slowly moves down with the ebbing tide and the sails are successively spread to the wind the compradore's san-pan is left behind, and as a last effort of good will the kindly Chinaman performs for the foreigners that religious ceremony which they show no inclination to perform for themselves. The basket of exploding crackers is raised aloft, the ghos-papers lighted, and a successful voyage is implored of the gods of the winds and waters by the clashing of the brazen gong.'

By the Treaty of Nanking which ended the first China war in 1842 Hong Kong was ceded to Britain and four ports besides Canton were opened to international trade. After the repeal of the Navigation Laws in 1849 there was as much hustle and bustle in these Treaty Ports as we complain of in our lives today. No time for courtesies. As the clippers, perhaps only just arrived, received their cargoes they loaded them at speed, for in effect this was passage time. The quicker the job was done the sooner they would be off and the better chance they would have of reaching the Port of London first.

At this period – though not formerly – it really was a case of racing the new season's teas to market. The first picking – *show-chum*, the 'first spring' – was made in mid-April. It was small and of high quality, two leaves and a bud. The second crop was picked early in June. By the middle of that month the tea would have reached at least one of the Treaty Ports. Foochow generally got it several weeks earlier than Canton or Shanghai so it became popular with the crack skippers.

The loading had to be done carefully because clippers with their fine lines were easily put out of trim, which reduced their speed. Also, tea is one of the most easily damaged of cargoes if air, water or fumes from the bilges get at it. None the less loading was done fast, for the Chinese stevedore was the best in the world. The quick little barefooted men knew their job inside out and worked with a will. First they prepared the hold. Clippers were permanently ballasted with about 100 tons

The Coast of China

of iron kentlage arranged on each side of the keelson. On top of this was laid clean, dry shingle (hard, not porous stone which might contain water). The shingle was rounded down from the middle outwards to leave an exactly equal space everywhere below the cambered deck. The Chinese would pick out a single stone which projected and might prevent the calculated number of layers of cases being fitted in, tightly but not too tight. Pairs of Chinamen loaded from the outside inwards, hammering the middle tea chest of each layer – as it were the keystone of the arch – into place with a wooden mallet. Every metal projection was dunnaged with planking, every space with plaited or split bamboo. Thus within a couple of days many thousands of tea chests were stowed by hand.

The distance between the alternative Chinese ports increased or reduced the homeward run by several hundred miles. Canton was the farthest south. About 400 miles to the north was Amoy, then Foochow. The anchorage of Foochow was off Pagoda Island, some twenty miles above the outer bar of the cliff-sided River Min, which was difficult to navigate. Shanghai, 1,000 miles north of Canton, was twelve miles up the River Whagpoo which flows into the Yangtze Kiang estuary at Woosung. To reach or leave Shanghai a clipper was not dependent upon tugs. But Hankow, only used in the later clipper days, was 900 miles up the Yangtze. Even downstream a five or six days' tow was necessary. In 1866 five out of seven ships got into trouble, one of them, the *Guinevere*, being lost. There were other dangers besides rocks and currents. The *Challenger*, the first ship to use Hankow – in 1863 – carried some missionaries as passengers to that town. The Chinese ate them.

So the general picture we get is of ships hurrying out from New York and London to one of half a dozen Chinese ports which might be as much as a thousand miles apart. Those loading at the same port would see each other there – it was unlikely that they did on the way out – but they could not know what loadings were taking place elsewhere. As quickly as possible the merchants bought the new teas and chartered cargo space in the most suitable vessel – not too quickly or they might get the remains of the last year's crop mixed into what they bought. Meanwhile the masters saw to their repairs.

Quickly but carefully they loaded, got their clearance papers and were away, knowing nothing – unless by some chance encounter at sea – of where they lay in the race, but racing for all they are worth for three months or more and perhaps first sighting their closest rival in the English Channel.

It was often said that the race was won or lost before reaching the Indian Ocean. It did not always prove so, but certainly the China Sea with its typhoons, its numerous islands and uncharted rocks, and the narrow channels which had to be negotiated put the heaviest tax upon a shipmaster's skill. It was, of course, no longer a case of waiting for the north-east monsoon. The clippers cut close hauled into the south-west wind. They were designed for it. The boldest went as straight as possible southwards through the China Sea, close to the land, and entered the Indian Ocean by the narrow strait between Sumatra and Java, at Anjer. The main alternative route, considerably longer, was out into the Pacific, outside the Philippines, and down past the island of Timor just north of Australia. After that, in either case, it was hell for leather for the Cape of Good Hope, the chief danger being the loss of spars or canvas from carrying too much sail. The Atlantic could be heartbreaking – calms or headwinds. Often there was a headwind in the Channel. And finally there was the gamble of getting a good tug exactly when it was wanted. But sometimes two clippers would go on racing for the Straits of Dover, tugs chugging beside them, demanding to be employed, and being told to sheer off before they got a bucket of water down the funnel.

The last half-day of the race was all that the landsmen could share before the days of the telegraph. In some ways this added to the excitement. There were months of hopes and conjecture, bets made in clubs, on Change or among friends at home. Then by semaphore from Start Point came news that, say, two or three tea ships were racing up the Channel. People on the south coast could watch them through telescopes – the raking masts, the enormous spread of canvas, the white waves peeling from the sharp bow, the figurehead leaning forward as if straining to get home.

Immediately there was bustle and excitement in the City. The brokers glanced at their weather clocks which told them the direction of the wind. Directly the ships were reported off Gravesend brokers and the sampling clerks rode hard to the docks. Directly the ship docked some cases were broken open for samples, or sample boxes were thrown ashore. They were rushed to Mincing Lane for the teas to be tasted, bid for, bought. By next morning they were on sale, not only in London but Liverpool and Manchester.

The winning crew received as much as £500 in prize money. The first tea of the season sold highest, not only for its quality. People liked to drink and offer their guests tea carried by a famous ship. In a way they thereby shared in its adventure.

III

The clipper races have been studied and recorded by Basil Lubbock, Arthur Clark, David McGreggor and others. Here, as an example, only one will be described – that of 1866 which is the most famous of them all although by that date there were no longer any American clippers free to compete. In that tea season at least forty British ships sailed from Chinese ports, sixteen from Foochow. Of these, five left the Pagoda Island anchorage within three days. This is the field to be considered:

Ariel, Captain Keay, was the favourite. She was a composite clipper (built of wood and iron) of 852 tons, and had been launched at Greenock in June the year before. Her sail area was of 25,451 square feet, the size of nine tennis courts. She excelled in light airs. Her only serious fault, being of extreme clipper design and with a very fine stern, was that she was apt to be pooped when running before a big wind. In fact that was probably her fate when she disappeared with all hands in 1872. She was a particularly slim and lovely ship, said to be capable of sixteen knots. In 1866 she had never been overtaken.

Taeping, 767 tons, Captain McKinnon, was also composite built, greenheart and teak on an iron frame. Her bowsprit and lower masts were of iron. She had been launched at Glasgow in 1863 and, like *Ariel*, excelled in light winds. On her maiden voyage she suffered considerable damage in a typhoon but after repair sailed from Amoy to Deal in eighty-eight days. In

The clippers *Ariel* and *Taeping*, racing up Channel in 1866.
From an oil painting by J. Spurling

A tea estate in Ceylon. The bushes grow among shade trees

1865 she took ninety-four days between London and Hong Kong. But on her outward voyage in 1866 she had lost her master and was under command of her mate, Dowdy.

Serica, 708 tons, Captain Innes, was a wooden clipper, launched the same year as *Taeping*, and sharper than she. Therefore she was less efficient in heavy weather. But she had won the race in 1864 and had other excellent runs to her credit. Her master had the reputation of being a hard driver.

Fiery Cross, 695 tons, Captain Robinson, was built in Liverpool of wood and launched in 1860. She had steel masts and patent reefing topsails. On the return passage of her maiden voyage she won the race and a 10s. premium per ton of cargo. She repeated this performance in 1862, 1863 and 1865. In 1864 she was only a day behind the winner, *Serica*. She also made three remarkable outward passages, two of ninety-two and one of ninety days, while on the outward passage of this year, 1866, she had overtaken *Serica*. No ship afloat boasted a better record.

Taitsing, 815 tons, Captain Nutsford, was a composite clipper, launched at Glasgow in 1865, a month after *Ariel* which ship she somewhat resembled, though she looked heavier built. She had had little time to show her paces but her master was known as a hard driver. On her maiden voyage she sailed from the Downs to Hong Kong in ninety-six days.

In the race to be described each of these ships carried over a million pounds of tea (at a freight of £7 a ton). Towards the end of May they were taking it aboard at the Pagoda Island anchorage, eleven miles below Foochow and twenty-two above the outer bar of the river Min.

Ariel, favoured by the merchants because she was the favourite, settled her business first, finished loading first and was off down the rapid, narrow, cliff-girt river with the paddle tug *Island Queen* alongside at 5 p.m. on 28 May. But this tug proved insufficiently powerful to control her in the tidal water, and she had to wait twenty-four hours for another. How maddening this must have been after a good start!

Fiery Cross, after her outward passage, had made a coastal voyage to Rangoon and had only very recently reached Foochow where she was loading with the greatest possible speed, along with the other ships. Captain Robinson, seeing

147

Ariel start, scrambled the rest of his cargo on board and left without his papers and without signing his bills of lading, twelve hours before the rest of the field. He was lucky in his tug and passed *Ariel* at anchor inside the bar, thus gaining a fourteen hours' lead.

Captain Innes of *Serica*, it is said, was driven nearly mad with vexation by Robinson's action. *Serica* and *Taeping* got away almost together and left the river mouth with *Ariel* at about 10.30 next morning. *Taitsing* sailed next day, followed by five other clippers which never had a chance in the race.

Fiery Cross more than kept her lead on the run down the China Sea. She passed Anjer after only twenty days and entered the Indian Ocean a day or more ahead of the rest. The order of the other four was then *Ariel, Taeping, Serica, Taitsing*.

Across the Indian Ocean all five ships made fast runs, *Ariel* once logging 330 miles in a day, and *Fiery Cross* 328 miles. *Taitsing* was gradually catching up. Every stitch of canvas was piled on.

At the Cape *Ariel* was only two hours behind *Fiery Cross*, *Taeping* fourteen. In the Atlantic the field closed up, but not enough for the ships to be in sight one from another. They raced on without knowing their relative positions. At St Helena, the order was *Taeping, Fiery Cross, Serica, Ariel, Taitsing*.

Then *Ariel* began to catch up. At Ascension Island she had overhauled *Serica*. *Ariel, Fiery Cross* and *Taeping* crossed the Equator together on 4 August. *Serica* had by then dropped two days behind, and *Taitsing* eight.

North of the line, *Ariel* swung farther westward than her two close rivals. *Taeping* and *Fiery Cross* remained in sight of each other for thirteen days. They were now in the Doldrums and here *Fiery Cross* had a stroke of bad luck. She was becalmed. But *Taeping*, though close, picked up a light breeze and sailed out of sight in five hours. *Fiery Cross* remained virtually motionless for twenty hours longer.

Meanwhile *Ariel*, so good in light airs, had forged ahead. She passed the Cape Verde Islands on 12 August, a day ahead of *Taeping* and *Fiery Cross*, and of *Serica* which had caught up with them. *Taitsing* was still last but had made up two days since crossing the Equator.

The first four ships passed Flores in the Azores on 29 August, *Ariel* still leading. By brilliant sailing *Taitsing* had made up another three days.

From then on the winds were generally fresh and favourable, and the speeds high. The ships were never far apart. *Ariel* was first to see the Bishop Light. But *Taeping* was close on her heels. On 5 September these two ships were racing up the Channel together neck and neck at fourteen knots. There was only ten minutes between them at the Downs, which *Ariel* signalled on 6 September, ninety-nine days out. The remaining three reached the Downs, *Serica* at noon on the same day, *Fiery Cross* during the night of 7 September and *Taitsing* on the morning of 9 September, 101 days out.

But the race was not yet over. It would end when the first crew threw their sample boxes ashore in the docks. And for the end of the race, as for the beginning, they depended on tugs.

This best of races had the most unsatisfactory end, yet there was something grimly appropriate in it.

Taeping, though lying second, got the first tug. It was some time before another came out to *Ariel*, and it was a less powerful one.

At Gravesend *Taeping* was fifty-five minutes ahead. Nonetheless, *Ariel* reached the Blackwall and East India Dock first, at 9 p.m. – but because of the tide could not enter it. *Taeping* had farther to go to the London Docks. She reached there an hour later and, drawing less water than her rival, managed to get in at three minutes past ten. *Ariel* did not dock until 10.23 p.m. So, technically, *Taeping* won by twenty minutes.

Ever since the leaders had been sighted in the Channel there had been tremendous excitement in the City. News of their progress had been flashed from every headland. The owners of the two clippers, fearing a quibble over the result – as in fact there was – got together and decided to split the bonus. So neither won.

The truth is that the clipper which first got a good steam tug won the race. It was a clear sign that steam was soon to drive the sailing ships from the seas.

.   .   .   .   .

In 1870, the first season after the Suez Canal was opened, the ports of China were crowded not only with clippers but also a larger number of steamships, looking awkward and ugly as uncouth adolescents among the stately sailing vessels.

The tea crop that year was abundant. There were more cargoes than usual to be loaded. But the merchants gave none to the clippers. They loaded all the new tea on the steamers at £4 10s a ton plus 10s for the first ship home. Not even then were they faster than the best clippers, for they had to stop *en route* to refuel, but they were the latest thing.

The best the clippers could pick up were cargoes for Australia at £1 10s to £2 10s a ton.

CHAPTER IX

Tea in Public and in Private

Nowhere is the English genius of domesticity
more notably evidenced than in the festival of
afternoon tea.

George Gissing

COFFEE, that friendly old bean, came first and established
coffee houses. These served as bridgeheads for the invasion of
tea. What they evolved into has affected the Englishman's
urban life ever since.

It is a peculiarity of the British as opposed to the Latin races
that they cannot comfortably talk without something to eat
or drink. They could talk in taverns, of course, but there, as
Shen Nung had put it a few thousand years earlier, they might
say foolish things and repent thereof in sober moments. The
coffee houses, where all classes met in an otherwise most class-
conscious age, were ideal for conversation. Coffee and tea
were both available, with pipes and tobacco to go with them.
Clear brains were prompted to exchange ideas freely and on
any subject.

Too freely for Charles II, who, in 1675, issued a Proclamation to suppress coffee houses as 'nurseries of idleness and
pragmaticalness'. But it was never made effective. The King
realized that the opposition would be too strong. So these
pleasant meeting places which had begun to flourish under the
Commonwealth (Garway's advertisement of tea at the *Sultaness
Head* appeared in the issue of the *Gazette* which announced
Cromwell's death), survived the Stuarts' second innings and
continued until the middle of the eighteenth century. At one

time there were as many as 2,000 coffee houses in London alone. This boom emptied the taverns and inclined the revenue to make up its losses on alcohol by higher and higher duties on tea.

The clients gave character to individual coffee houses. So Whigs were found in one, Tories in another, poets in a third and clergy in a fourth. Men of fashion came to congregate at White's in St James's, business men at Lloyd's, while Tom's in Devereux Court was associated with the law and the business side of tea. White's became the club it is, Lloyd's the heart of insurance, and Tom's housed the tea-trader Thomas Twining until from lack of space he moved next door to the *Golden Lion* which was to be the first shop exclusively dedicated to the sale of tea. From these examples it will be seen that the coffee houses did not die, but having served their purpose changed to something else.

Coffee houses helped to establish tea as the national beverage. Smuggling, the other helper, took it to the home. There are several things that Englishmen like to do without their womenfolk (yet without any lack of love for them), but drinking tea is not one of those things – quite the reverse. Tea without a lady to pour it is mere self-indulgence. So men took tea at home. The next stage was equally logical, or at least inevitable. Housewife and maiden wanted to be taken out – to tea in tea-gardens which evolved from existing pleasure gardens. There one might see and be seen by the gay world. Edward Young wrote:

> Her two red lips affected zephyrs blow
> To cool the Bohea and inflame the Beau;
> While one white finger and a thumb conspire
> To lift the cup and make the world admire.

The tea-gardens were in the country – in Chelsea, Bayswater, Hampstead, Marylebone and elsewhere in the then green belt around the then slim town. They consisted of formal flower-beds, shrubberies and pools, winding paths for gentle exercise, and arbours ('genteel boxes') in which to whisper, rest and take refreshment. There were buildings too – in case the weather should not be fine.

The gardens were open from May to September. In the

evenings they were gaily lighted with thousands of lanterns. There were concerts and firework displays. Tea-gardens catered for every stratum of society, from royalty to the kitchen maid and her young man. As with coffee houses there was little or no class distinction here. Tea-gardens were not expensive. The inclusive charge was generally sixpence or a shilling. Ranelagh cost half a crown. It offered an 'elegant regale', which meant tea with bread and butter.

As with coffee houses and clubs each tea-garden acquired from its clients individual characteristics. They all *tried* to be genteel and some of them unfortunately succeeded. Some, like Bermondsey Spa and Sadler's Wells, offered supposedly salutary waters as well as tea. Bagnigge Wells was bourgeois.

> Bone Tone's the space twixt Saturday and Monday.
> And riding in a one-horse chais on Sunday.
> 'Tis drinking tea on summer afternoons
> At Bagnigge Wells with china and gilt spoons.

Cooper's Gardens, just across Waterloo Bridge, was called Cupid's Garden:

> ... Tea and wine
> Here you may have, and also dine;
> But as you through the garden rove
> Beware, fond youths, the darts of love.

At every tea-garden you could get into trouble if you wanted to. Vauxhall claimed that even Bishops could be seen in the gardens without injury to their reputations. *Qui s'excuse, s'accuse*. Those gentlemen visitors to the White Conduit House developed a technique of treading on a lady's train, apologizing humbly and offering her a cup of tea.

> While tea and cream and butter'd rolls can please,
> While rival beaux and jealous belles exist,
> So long, White Conduit House, shall be thy fame,'

said the *Gentleman's Magazine*.

At the Parthenon gardens the ladies were inclined to take the initiative with the pretty phrase: 'Pray sir, will you treat me to a dish of tea?'

New York had its tea-gardens just outside the town, two

153

of them named after London's Ranelagh and Vauxhall. But in both countries they were restricted or overwhelmed during the first half of the nineteenth century by the spread of the towns. The buildings, shorn of their gardens which had been four or five acres in extent, turned into taverns or were pulled down.

Then for about thirty years – the time span of a generation – there was nowhere to go out to tea, unless one could afford one of the few and fashionable establishments like Gunters. The fun had gone. Tea in other people's houses is more often a social duty than a treat. Social calls, temperance tea meetings – there must have been talk about the good old days!

At last in 1884 there was an innovation which, looking back on it, seems so obvious that it is difficult to understand why nobody had thought of it long before. Yet apparently nobody did until the kindly manageress of the Aerated Bread Company's shop near London Bridge put the idea up to the directors. She used to give a cup of tea in her room at the back to a few old customers when they came off the train or looked in to buy bread. They were so appreciative of this that she thought it might be a good idea to sell tea to drink on the premises. The directors approved. The first teashop was opened. It was a success from the start. Within ten years the Express Dairy and Lyons were following suit on an ever-increasing scale.

It is impossible to believe that the era of the teashop will ever end – unless a utopian government of the future provides free tea for all the people all the time. In offices and factories tea, as everybody knows, is an integral part of the productive day. Management does not try to interfere, not merely because this would cause a strike – as has happened – but because experience has shown that the English worker without tea is like an engine without oil – which does not necessarily work if you give it some but certainly does not if you don't.

II

The importance of tea to a household may be judged by the tea-things of that house. Not only tea but china came from China. Pots and cups of the same light, beautiful ware were soon demanded by those who bought the expensive herb. For tea had to have its elegant retinue – its service, or 'equipage' as it came to be called. But European potters did not know the age-old secret of Chinese porcelain, nor of china in general, and it took them some time to discover it by trial and elimination. The urgent demand for elegant utensils for tea in fashionable houses proved a valuable incentive not only to English potters but our silversmiths too. Silver we did know how to work, and tea was an entirely new field in which skill and craftsmanship could be displayed. The first known English tea pot carries the date 1670 with the inscription, 'This silver tea pott was presented to ye Comtee of ye East India Company by ye Honoe George Lord Berkeley of Berkeley Castle A member of that Honorable and worthy Society, and A true lover of them'. (This formal use of the word lover was not unusual. John Company used to end its letters, even those of severe criticism, with the phrase, 'Your loving friend'.) This tea pot looks exactly like a coffee pot – a truncated cone, the straight spout at right angles to the handle in the horizontal plane.

Silver tea pots soon broke away from the coffee pot design. The tapered spout became curved, the body pear-shaped. But for a hundred years or more tea pots were simple in design, even when other shapes – octagonal and oval – were introduced. Spoons, milk jug, sugar bowl and tongs made up a matching set. In the eighteenth century our silversmiths were at their very best. Gradually thereafter rococo and Victorian ornamentation increased. Now silver tea pots are returning to the simplicity of their youth. Fortunately they are not easily destroyed so one can follow the whole evolution of this purely occidental art which is almost exactly as old as tea-drinking in the West.

In China the fragile, handle-less cup is as old as porcelain, dating back to the days of China's true greatness. But tea pots are for that country a comparatively modern invention. There was no need of them, for tea was made by throwing the dry leaves into a boiling cauldron or pouring boiling water on to leaves in the cup. The ewers with spouts, in something like the shape of a tea pot, which were made long before the year A.D. 1500 were almost certainly only used for wine. Not until

1500 did the Chinese begin to make red or brown unglazed stoneware tea pots at Yi-Hsing, famous for its clay. It was said that these heat-resisting containers made the best tea. The pots were small, so that each person could have his own. They were beautiful when simple but ridiculous when ornate – made to look like tortoises or elephants' trunks or something else equally far removed from their purpose in life. They came to Europe with the early imports of tea – as the quotation from Marlow's voyages on page 126 shows.

The Dutch potters had a certain start in china-making for they had first tried to copy Chinese utensils serviceable for cold liquids. In Delft they already made stoneware, which is clay heated to a temperature at which it becomes vitrified and impervious – as opposed to earthenware which is pervious to water. But the first Delft tea pots lacked the heat-resisting qualities of the Yi-Hsing, so the Dutch potters set themselves to copy the Chinese, and from a purely practical – not artistic – point of view they succeeded.

Two Dutchmen, John and Philip Elers, also made unglazed red earthenware tea pots in Fulham, and later in Staffordshire where the best clay is found. But during the first half of the eighteenth century English pottery scarcely advanced because it could not rival silverware in either beauty or efficiency. Wedgwood was the first great name in pottery. In partnership with Whieldon, Josiah Wedgwood made 'jasper' ware of variously coloured stone ware decorated with the white cameo reliefs which are still famous. With this innovation Staffordshire pottery soared in both quality and quantity, and such brilliant artists as Flaxman were drawn in to improve design.

The next stage was porcelain. It will make description clearer if one anticipates the knowledge of the potters of the period by giving definitions. Soft paste porcelain is made principally of white clay, powdered glass and bone ash. Compared to hard paste it is fired at a low temperature. Hard paste, the true translucent porcelain, is a mixture of infusible china clay and fusible china stone. At St Cloud in France they were making soft paste before the end of the seventeenth century. Hard paste was made by Böttger at Meissen in 1713. Soon Bottger was producing matching breakfast sets complete with porcelain tray. England was far behind but came plodding up for her usual late success in the latter half of the eighteenth century. That was when Chelsea, Bow, Derby, Worcester earned the right to be household words.

It is an intriguing thought that all these beautiful and delicate accessories of tea were being gradually evolved while smugglers and revenue officers were knocking each other about so roughly.

There was another contrast even more striking. While the great mass of the Chinese nation was passing on from generation to generation its hatred of the foreign devils, and while the European merchants in Canton were treating with a patronizing amusement those officials with whom they dealt, English fashionable society was striving to imitate everything Chinese, at least what was artistic and concerned with tea – lacquer tables and trays, Chinese screens and motifs in the tea-room.

A striking example is willow pattern china which can still be seen everywhere. It is said to have been first made at Caughley in Shropshire. The designs tell a Chinese tale which in the hands of various makers varies slightly but in general is as follows. Koong-Se is a beautiful heiress who lives in a house in the centre of the pattern. The garden has the usual weeping willow tree and little hump-back bridge. She is in love with her father's secretary, Chang. Father is very angry about this. He orders Chang away, and promises Koong-Se to a wealthy and debauched nobleman. He builds a fence across the foreground of the pattern and confines his daughter to the garden which is encircled by the stream.

But love finds out a way. Chang floats messages down the river in a coconut shell, and Koong-Se recovers them.

The rich suitor is invited to the house and gives Koong-Se a box of jewels. But at the feast which follows he gets drunk and Chang manages to enter the house disguised as a beggar. He signs to Koong-Se, and off they go. Three figures run across the bridge – Koong-Se with a distaff, the sign of virginity, Chang with the box of jewels, a sign of good sense, and angry father with a stick.

Chang hides Koong-Se while he goes for a boat. He returns with it just in time to take her away before her father's guards close in. They drift a long way down the river. They build a house and Chang tills the ground, every inch of it, in his thorough Chinese way. The lovers do not live happy ever after, for Chang is foolish enough to become an author and his fame spreads far and wide. Thus the nobleman finds him and has him killed by his soldiers. The distracted Koong-Se burns down the house on top of herself. The judgement of the gods is that the nobleman is cursed and the lovers are transformed into doves to take up their final and decorative place in the upper part of the pattern.

In America pottery was started by English workmen following English methods and designs. But it was not long before Americans were making their own china with conspicuous success at Trenton and Flemington, at East Liverpool, Zanesville and Cincinnatti, and at Syracuse. Such charming and lovable tea services did these potteries produce that it must have been very hard indeed for patriotic ladies to banish every sign and trace of the 'pernicious herb' from their houses. One wrote a sad little ode of farewell to tea and her tea equipage.

> Cups and saucers, cream jug, sugar tongs,
> And pretty tea chest also.

In spite of the early Occidental wish to copy all things Chinese, most of the utensils which we think of as necessary for the proper service of tea are of purely Western origin. Tea-spoons, sugar bowl and tongs, milk or cream jug, saucers, caddies (which locked like money-boxes when tea was expensive) – the Chinese never had use for any of these. Nor had they for the kindliest and most useful adjuncts of them all – the tea cosy.

CHAPTER X

Gardens Old and New

Tea is a work of art and needs a master hand to
bring out its noblest qualities.

Okakura-Kakuzo

TEA – like wine but little else – is produced from raw material
to finished product by a single staff on the same site. (Blending
is done elsewhere. But this, like mixing a cocktail, is a com-
bining of finished products.) Cultivation merges into manufacture.

In China these processes have hardly changed since the
time of Lu Yu when the sun dried the leaves, charcoal fired
them and hands or feet were used to roll them. But in gardens
elsewhere science soon raised its functional head. Production
by Europeans is only about 130 years old. We will glance at
it in the early days, the middle days, and finally look more
closely at the present.

For the Dutch in Java and the British in Assam it started
with imported Chinese labour. When the Europeans lost
this help the interest begins. Most contemporary accounts
are dry records of achievement, the people concerned being
too busy or bothered to describe the human side of their
work and the day-to-day struggle with nature. But a little of
this comes out here and there and will be used to paint the
picture.

In Assam a main difficulty was labour. In the mid-nineteenth
century, a vast amount of very heavy labour was required to
make tea-gardens out of virgin jungle. The local Nagas were
unequalled as head-hunters but not to be depended upon as

cultivators. They were described by a Victorian planter as 'quite uncivilized . . . I saw a party of these savages feast on (and in) an elephant many days deceased . . . The full national costume consists of merely pieces of coloured cane wound round the small of the calf and round the waist'.

These tribesmen were useful, however, for the first destructive phase of cultivation.

'It is a sight well worth watching to see a gang of Nagas extended in a line against the jungle they are clearing, cleaving their way steadily and surely through the dense undergrowth and bamboo jungle, dexterously swinging their peculiarly-shaped daos (half axe, half sword) in unison and in time with the barbarous refrain of some war song which they continually chant in their wild and unintelligible jargon. . . .

'When the land has had all the jungle cut down and burnt or dragged away the ground is well hoed up, which is very hard work on account of the network of roots in the earth. The clods are then broken up, and the soil pulverized by women armed with truncheons, and all roots, runners, etc., must be extracted and thrown away.'

Dwelling houses were constructed on stilts to be clear of the *mal'aria*. (This habit was maintained, for although the anopheles mosquito could enter, snakes were kept out.) Roads were cut to the river which was the only means of long-distance communication until single-track railways began to penetrate the jungle.

Apart from a natural disinclination to work for any length of time, the Nagas and the other local peoples – Mishmis, Meris, Fakiyols – were too few in that scarcely populated land to provide a labour corps for the ever-increasing gardens. So labour had to be imported from India. The collection, transport, housing and general management of coolies who were as foreign to Assam as were the planters themselves caused endless trouble which continued through several decades at least. (The Ceylon planters have also had to depend on imported labour. They have been fortunate in being able to obtain good coolies by recruiting Tamils from southern India.) Well-meaning people with more or less justification protested at the mortality of coolies on the road or on the plantations. But published statistics gave an inaccurate impression, for they generally concealed the fact that these people had a high death rate in their home villages.

Recruiting, however, provided cause for complaint. A planter, David Crole, wrote:

'There are two systems of recruiting, namely *arcutti* and *sirdari*. By the former method Coolies are collected (from the poorest districts of India) by professional recruiters (not very scrupulous rogues as may well be imagined) and massed in large depots from which they are literally purchased by planters or their agents in batches varying from half a dozen to a score or two, at a price averaging about ninety rupees per head for a good batch.'

When 'purchased' they signed indentures, which a magistrate explained to them, to work for four or five years.

The second method was to send a trusted coolie back to his own village for a few months to collect recruits by personal persuasion. This was found preferable.

Coolies were of both sexes. The men were expected to learn their work of cultivation within a year. They were found easier to handle than the women, who were, and still are, employed in plucking the bushes. As early as 1890 there were patent plucking machines on the market but to this day nothing has been evolved as efficient as the delicate female hand. Female ingenuity, however, could be troublesome. The women were paid for the weight of leaf they picked, so: 'She often immerses her basket of leaf bodily in a pool of water, or puts a soaking wet cloth, or even sheets of lead foil (purloined from the packing-room of the factory) into the bottom of her basket, sometimes hiding it with a cunningly devised false bottom.' But these were the black sheep. Others increased their basic pay by industry. 'Many good workers earn double pay during the height of the season, and such are eagerly sought after by the coolie men.'

From this comes a glimpse of the patriarchal position assumed by the Victorian planter. At the end of the day he notices a woman standing shyly at the foot of his veranda steps.

'"Well, who are you?"
'"I am Rai, Sahib."

'"What do you want? Leave?"'

'"No, I don't want anything, Sahib."'

'"Well, if that's all you won't have much difficulty in getting it."'

'The woman remains standing as before. Orientals, however nervous, do not fidget with their hands. But this woman, with modestly bowed head, is drawing patterns with her foot. At last she confesses:

'"I want a husband."

"Oh! Well, who is he?"

'"Lutchman."

'"Where is he? Why doesn't he come himself?"

'A man may now be noticed slinking up towards the bungalow in a very shamefaced way.

'"You are Lutchman, eh?"

'"Huzzur!"

'"Do you wont Rai as your wife?"

'"Yes, Sahib."

'"And do you want Lutchman as your husband, Rai?"

'"Yes, Sahib."

'"Well, I don't see any objection. You are both good coolies, and work well. But just mark what I say: you must live amicably together. I won't have any brawling in the lines on any account. . . ."''

So it was settled. That night the friends and relations held a little celebration and the couple moved into the same thatched hut, or rather the same quarter of a partitioned hut which they shared with three or more other families. They had a small vegetable garden and grazing for a buffalo or two.

In due course children appeared, 'Strange, solemn-looking, old-fashioned mites, and very precocious'. At the age of five or six they started work, helping their mothers pluck, at 3s a month. Later they were employed in catching crickets and grubs, later still in the withering sheds and factory. (Here the word is used in its modern sense, a place where something is made.) At sixteen they earned an adult's wage.

There was no school, but there was a hospital, run by a 'doctor babu', where invalids were nursed by their relations.

It sounds a fairly benign patriarchy. Mr Crole said, 'I am

sure that a policy of reasonable kindness and conciliation is never thrown away on any sentient being.' But there were abuses. For instance, when coolies married it was most unlikely that their respective contracts had the same time to run. If the man's expired first he might be told that he must go, leaving his wife behind, unless he renewed his contract. When the woman's expired she would be faced with the same choice. So they both had to remain for life, or separate.

Recreational welfare went no farther than the issue – only because tradition demanded it – of a bottle of rum once a year to assist the celebration of the Fagua festival. The result is thus described.

'The coolie is not at all a bad fellow in many ways, but were he judged only from what one sees of him during his carnival of drink and lust, he would, I fear, be for ever condemned. It is not a nice sight, but a fearful one, to see the flickering fire and dying torches, just before the dawn, light up the glistening naked bodies and starting eyes of a score of dusky satyrs and mænads assailing the serenity of the heavens with their drunken frenzy and licentiousness, and making the night air quiver with their raucous and mirthless shouts, while in the gloom, surrounding the circle of fitful light, lie insensible the inert bodies of those who have already succumbed to the effects of the maddening liquor and bacchanalian riot. One cannot imagine a better picture of "hell let loose".

'Part of the rites of the Fagua festival consists in the votaries of the god smearing themselves and those connected with them, or whom they wish to honour, with a magenta-coloured powder. The custom is an unpleasant one in itself to the European, but when its true and original signification is known, one is horribly disgusted.

'One is glad to record that a healthy determination seems to have set in amongst planters to curb, as far as lies in their power, the wanton licence and depravity practised in their gardens on such occasions. . . .

'The "nautch" (dance) is a great institution amongst coolies . . . Reformers have been turning their attention to the eradication of the custom of employing nautch girls as a necessary concomitant of any festival in national or private life. How far they are in earnest, or with what measure of success their efforts will meet, is for the future to disclose.'

Let us see what the future held – regarding welfare and technical improvement – by glancing at an Assam garden some forty years later, and then at gardens in general another forty years on, which will bring us to the present day. The middle period shows that techniques were little altered but that personal relations between employers and employed were much improved.

A. R. Ramsden went out to Assam in the early 1920s. He had been born there, the son of a planter, but schooling in England and the First World War had intervened and he returned as a novice to learn the job. His small book, *Assam Planter*, is of its sort quite excellent, and unfortunately long out of print.

On his first morning he was taken by his Cicero, Jack, to see the men who had been hoeing among the dew-dripping tea-bushes since first light. Then, after a visit to the hospital, where they saw a case of leprosy, a case of anthrax and a baby dying of convulsions:

'We went to see the women start the work of plucking. They were trooping up from the coolie lines – the tin shanties where they lived – in single file, each carrying a large basket on her head. In the shade at one end of a twelve-acre block of tea ready to be plucked they halted and put down their baskets. Each woman had to pluck three rows of tea 240 yards long. This meant one hundred and sixty women to every twelve acres. The best pluckers jealously defended their right to the same three rows in every block as by good plucking the yield could be considerably increased. . . .

'As we forged our way through the more than waist-high dripping wet tea, Jack corrected a woman here and there, cracked jokes with them mostly of the rather robust kind, and asked about their families and such things as the rice prospects on their holdings. Although he had only been in the country eighteen months, I was lucky to have him to show me the ropes. He had the natives feeding out of his hand and could raise a laugh or a smile out of them at any time, which is the way to handle native labour.

'Back at the bungalow we changed and had breakfast, a substantial meal as it was too hot at lunch-time to eat much. By then the men had finished their daily hoeing task and were turning out to the work of plucking green leaf. Each man carried two baskets hung from the ends of a whippy bamboo slung across his shoulders, and being empty they bounced up and down as he almost ran in his eagerness to start work, for it was considered overtime and paid for daily in cash at so much per seer (2½ lbs.) of green leaf. This meant more supervision for us, and we went through the long lines of men, women and children plucking the lower and younger tea-bushes.

'At midday the factory hooter gave a long drawn-out boom. Quite leisurely the women came out of the tea, helped each other to lift the baskets full of leaf on to their heads, and with the sirdars leading walked in single file towards the factory, moving with all the natural grace of the native woman accustomed to carrying heavy loads thus. Jack and I jumped on to our bicycles and rode on ahead of them to the withering houses, where we supervised the weighing of the green leaf, calling out in Hindustani ourselves the various amounts registered on the scales for a babu to write it up on a board. As the women one after another had their baskets weighed, they emptied them on to the withering racks, where the green leaf was thinly spread by small boys with long thin almost whiplash bamboos. I noticed that when they came up to weigh-in they walked through large shallow concrete tanks containing a solution of permanganate of potash.

'"What's the big idea, Jack?" I asked.

'"Oh, that's an attempt to keep down the hookworm incidence."'

When Ramsden had learned the ropes he was given the task of bringing a new garden into cultivation. First there were 250 acres of jungle to be cleared. Naga tribesmen were again used – on contract at Rs 35 an acre. Methods were much the same as before except that an Australian stump puller was used to get the big trunks out of the ground.

Then came road-making. Ramsden's description of the soil would make a gardener at home sigh with envy and a road-maker with despair – five or six feet depth of very rich loam on top of sand. Hardcore from other tea factories was dumped by the ton and a brick kiln built on the nearest patch of clay.

The road was not ready for traffic for a long time, but in February, four months after felling, the jungle trees and under-growth were dry enough to burn. Out of the roaring flames rose millions of winged insects, and tens of thousands of birds swooped over the smoke to feed on them. A host of snakes came gliding out with heads erect, to be attacked by Nagas armed with sticks.

After the burning only the hardwood trunks remained. These were sawn for timber on the spot by Nepalese sawyers working in pairs.

As each 12-acre block was completely cleared it was planted out with tea saplings, 4 feet 6 inches apart in each direction. Only the sites of ant-heaps could not be used because the soil was barren of bacteria. Transplanting continued until April, and then the old women and children lightly hoed the ground about the plants. These were, of course, much too young for plucking – on a new garden it is four years before the leaves are worth manufacturing – so building work began.

Ramsden had been allowed the equivalent of £225 for construction of his bungalow. With twenty-five Nagas, twenty-five coolies, the stump puller and an elephant he cleared the site for house and garden in a day. Up went the bungalow, to his own design, using local timber and local labour even for the furniture.

'I loved that bungalow more than any of the other habitations I have infested before or since. It fitted me exactly, and above all it spelt freedom with a capital F. . .'. With a good dog and no lack of books from home the talk of loneliness out in the jungle being bad for a man and sending him slightly crackers is absolute nonsense . . . I had more than enough to keep my mind occupied.'

In that forcing climate and rich soil where one species of bamboo is said to grow eighteen inches in a day and a night, what a garden sprang up almost while he watched it! Magnolias, gardenias, crotons, syringas, poinsettias, cannas, orchids grafted to every tree, fruit in abundance, flame-trees, hibiscus –it made him homesick for the soft shades of an English garden.

Twelve acres of thatch grass for the coolies' huts were planted out and work began in the factory, where they would deal with the leaves of the newly planted bushes when they were old enough.

Until the road was fit for use all heavy work was done by elephants. Ramsden liked elephants.

'As temperamental as a racehorse, as placid as a pumpkin, as blind as a bat and as clumsy as a camel, the elephant is very lovable in spite of being as savage as a hell cat. Not the sort of animal to have about the house, you might well say; but the elephant nevertheless inspires much genuine affection and is far more reliable than many of your women friends.'

At times the planter's work occupied eighteen hours of the twenty-four, but between whiles Ramsden got plenty of big-game shooting – tiger, crocodile, rogue elephants – and once a very original type of shoot. His Nepalese sawyers who lived in groups of two men and one woman got very drunk each week-end. Soon his new coolies began behaving similarly. Evidence suggested that the Nepalese were distilling liquor from rice beer and selling it to the coolies. To bring in the police would have given the garden a bad name and put a stop to recruiting in the future.

Mathaloo, Ramsden's personal servant and a great hunter, discovered the still. Near a spring in the jungle one of the Nepalese, assisted by a group of women, was making the stuff with fourteen four-gallon kerosene tins as the basic apparatus. 'If you want to shoot the man, Sahib, it will be quite easy,' Mathaloo said.

Ramsden took his rifle, and Mathaloo guided him to the place, making a wide detour through the jungle. Lying concealed, they saw:

'Fourteen kerosene tins were simmering on fourteen little fires. The tops were covered with huge thick leaves the shape of rhubarb leaves, but much thicker, cooler and smoother. A most ingenious funnel had also been made out of them, which caused the steam to condense, and I saw the drip, drip, drip into some little brass bowls underneath. A man sitting on his hunkers and obviously half drunk was superintending operations, and some women were fetching water, and emptying the bowls into bottles. All this was being done very quietly and unsuspiciously.

'I took careful aim. Crack! The first tin spouted on two sides. The man looked up stupidly, and the women were horribly scared. Then I fired rapidly along the line of tins, and they all ran like frightened deer, the long trailing voluminous skirts of the women flying in the wind.

'That effectively stopped the illicit distilling. When I returned to the garden I never said a word to anyone about it, and there was no need for punishment.'

The festival of Fagua (or Phagooa) was still observed. But the description was by that date shorter and less shocked. 'It means a monumental boose-up, the drinking of lau-pani (rice beer) is treated as a ritual and most of the coolies are drunk on the last day of the festival. There was always a busy office day and many cases in hospital after Phagooa.'

Gone are the lurid tales of nautch girls and pagan rites. Tea-growing in the 1920s as Ramsden paints it was man management, common sense, periods of real hard work interspersed with energetic sport. Blackwater fever took him away from it.

II

Over 100 years of experiment and consequent improvements have gone into the development of the modern tea estate, which is a garden and factory combined. No aspect – horticultural, chemical, social – has been allowed to stand still.

The modern tea-garden is a self-contained estate of anything between 100 and 2,000 acres. The dark green sea of bushes is cut by roads and tracks and dotted with white buildings – housing for the permanent labour force, the factory, a large, imposing structure, bungalows for senior and subordinate staff, offices and store house, the hospital, the school. Many of the clerical and supervising staff are natives now. The garden may be little above sea level or at an altitude of up to 7,000 feet. If the ground is flat the bushes are set out with geometrical precision, but on steep slopes each row of bushes follows a contour.

Let us take an acre and examine it. Some 3,000 bushes grow in that area and will absorb ten tons of water a day. A statistic which proves progress is that whereas an acre in Assam 100 years ago produced 300 lb of tea it now produces up to 1,500 lb. In Japan as much as 3,000 lb is harvested, but this is in return for 400 lb of nitrogen, 100 lb of phosphoric acid and 200 lb of potash. It takes two men to cultivate an acre and about five women to pluck it in full season, the number varying with the yield. (Each woman plucks 40 to 60 lb a day.) A 1,000-acre estate of average yield needs for garden and factory at least 1,500 workers.

At once one wonders if this heavy employment could not be reduced. In the factory mechanization is almost complete, in the garden almost non-existent. Weeding is generally done by hand. As for plucking, in Japan a sort of pelican's beak shears are used which cut and bag the shoots. A woman using these can increase her plucking to 250 lb a day. But a tenth of this consists of coarse leaf and twigs. In Georgia the Russians use a self-propelled machine which runs between bushes which are planted to form parallel hedges. It has a pneumatic comb with rubber-covered teeth which move against a static jaw and so break off the shoots. It gathers about the same proportion of coarse leaf and wood as do the Japanese shears.

Even if plucking machines were more efficient there would be arguments against their use. In most tea-producing areas labour is comparatively cheap because there are more people than jobs. But if it were grown in Australia, as has been suggested, or in the United States, where it was tried and discarded as uneconomic, mechanization would have to be complete. I feel pretty sure it never will be. Tea is too subtle a thing to be mechanized.

Linnaeus who invented double-barrelled Latin names for plants believed there were two kinds of tea-bush – *viridis* from which came green tea and *bohea* which gave black. Robert Fortune during his travels in China proved that green and black are made from the same sort of leaves by different methods of manufacture. Others confirmed this. So all the bushes in all the gardens are *Camellia sinensis*. But among the 3,000 bushes of the acre we were considering there are probably no two exactly alike. The ultimate cells of the tea-plant – as of every plant or animal – contain a number of thread-like things called chromosomes. Each chromosome (tea-plant cells have thirty-two) is made up of a number of genes which are the elements which transmit hereditary qualities – shape, habit, colour, tendency – of some part of the bush. Tea is not self-fertile. It must be pollinated by another plant. When that happens two lots of genes are shuffled together like two packs of cards and dealt out to the offspring just as they come. The offspring will probably inherit not only some qualities from each parent but also qualities of more or less distant ancestors which have been latent in the parents. The differences may not be great but where they concern quality and yield they are important. Sexual reproduction of tea-plants is about as chancy as it is with humans.

To reproduce a bush exactly it must be done vegetatively, by cuttings or layering. The importance of being able to do this was realized about 1930 when it was noticed that an individual bush might, though looking the same as all the rest, produce twice the crop of any other or a crop worth a shilling a pound more or less. To maintain the metaphor of the pack of cards, there had been a lucky deal. This could be repeated by leaf cuttings. But, of course, by selective cross-fertilization one *might* get a still luckier deal. So seeds are by no means out. In any case reproduction by seeds is much cheaper than by vegetative means.

The study of individual bushes was facilitated by the invention of a miniature rolling machine which deals with 2 oz of leaf. So, theoretically at least, the productivity of each bush can be checked as effectively as that of hens on an egg farm. At the same time visual study shows that the best quality producing plants have first and second leaves with abnormally hairy undersides. Thus, all the time, gardens are being 'derogued', to use the nice term employed by Mr Harler.

Another pleasant and descriptive term is 'kind' soil. Most soils are kind to the tea roots, provided they are acid. That of Assam is particularly kind. But for existence, as opposed to ample yield, tea will grow almost anywhere provided the climate is warm and wet. The Chinese use steep and rocky hillsides. One remembers the unlikely story of monkeys being used to pluck bushes growing on cliffs.

Tea will not grow for some time where lightning has struck, and bushes scorched by it must be uprooted for their roots are very liable to disease. Tea will not grow on the site of former human habitation. What it likes best of all is jungle soil.

Tea suffers sadly in a drought, but it can put up with almost any amount of rain, provided it is warm. At Nawalapitiya in that part of Ceylon which gets the full deluge of the south-west monsoon there is as much rain in June alone as we get in England in a year. Tea grows well there in quantity if not quality. Again and again one realizes that Dr Wallich was somehow not far out in his estimation of the requirements of good as opposed to the most common sort of tea.

In China and Japan tea is sown in its permanent position in the garden. In Chapter II you remember, an ancient authority was quoted as saying that as many as twelve seeds were planted in a single hole. This no doubt referred to Chinese circular planting, seeds being placed around the periphery of a circle eighteen inches in diameter. These make a composite bush of beehive shape.

Outside China and Japan tea nearly always starts its life in the nursery. When twelve to fifteen months old it is planted out at about 4-feet intervals unless the bushes are to form a hedge in which case the interval is less in the hedge-line. The hedge form, it is said, reduces damage to the bushes by the pluckers. Certainly that form will have to be used if ever mechanized plucking comes in.

Given space and no interference a tea-plant would grow into a conical tree at least 30 feet high and with pretty white flowers of the shape of the dog-rose. Instead – unless it is grown as a seed plant – it is ruthlessly pruned to make it sprout sideways and to keep it down to a height convenient for plucking in the form of a flat-topped bush. Plucking does not start for three years, longer at high altitudes where the plants grow more slowly – and produce better quality. The life of a tea-bush is about the same as ours, three score years and ten. After that, to avoid labour and sorrow, it is uprooted.

Fertilizers and green manure are forked in, but there are two points of view about weeding. Complete weeding looks nice and leaves all the food and water for the tea-plant, but a weed cover binds the soil and prevents erosion. Therefore 'selective weeding' is advocated – a phrase which might come in useful for the lazy flower gardener.

There are pests and diseases in plenty – the red spider, the tea mosquito bug, crickets, beetles, borers, caterpillars, thrips, mites and plenty of fungoid diseases. But they are all controllable by chemical sprays. These are excellent, yet somehow millions of tons of tea were produced before they were invented.

Near the equator, in Ceylon for instance, the bushes continue to grow and produce new leaves all the year round. The flushes are plucked every week or every fortnight, the higher the altitude the fewer the flushes. But in Assam, northern India and places of similar or higher altitude there is a close season between December and the end of March. The bushes, being evergreen, retain their leaves, but they don't grow. Leaves fit for tea-making must be young and vigorously growing, full of sap. The word 'flush' is perfectly descriptive of this sudden access of fresh green.

So we leave the garden with a picture of rich green, interspersed with the different tints of shade trees, and speckled with the bright garments of the pluckers, working with lightning fingers breast high among the bushes, or walking gracefully with the big baskets on their heads.

III

'Manufacture starts in the field,' it is said. That is literally true to the extent that good cultivation improves the yield and accurate or careless plucking affects the final product. But, besides, the aroma of tea is easily perceptible in the fields on a warm, damp day. A vineyard does not smell of wine. So one may deduce that the chemical changes in making tea are less drastic than those in making wine. Chiefly they bring out existing characteristics and leave the leaf in a state in which it is easily preserved.

There are three main methods of manufacture which, though starting with the same sort of leaf, end up with three strikingly different products – Black Tea, Green Tea and Oolong Tea. With Black Tea we are chiefly concerned, for that is what most of the world now drinks, so its manufacture will be fully described after dealing with the other two. Black Tea is completely fermented. Green Tea is not fermented at all. It is steamed, which makes the leaves sufficiently pliable to be rolled and prevents fermentation by inactivating the enzymes. After being steamed the leaf is alternately partially dried and rolled until it becomes too crisp to be manipulated. Thereafter it is fully dried. The secret here is the killing by heat at the *start* of the process. The Chinese often do this by heating in a hot pan instead of by steaming. The process with pictures described in Chapter II was evidently of Green Tea making.

Oolong Tea is bruised by manipulation, which sets fermentation going. But before this is completed (as in Black Tea) the leaf is killed by roasting. The full Chinese process is highly elaborate, starting with semi-drying and manipulation in the field and ending with alternate rolling and roasting in the factory. Oolong finds a small market in the United States but elsewhere is now only drunk in China and Formosa.

When we started making Black Tea in India we followed the Chinese method, knowing no other. Though elaborate and complex it is worth a brief mention for out of it modern methods evolved. Directly the leaves had been plucked they were spread out in the sun, being turned by hand all the while. Then they were spread out in the shade for half an hour, then manipulated and gently rolled – always by hand. This cracked the surface, exposing the cells and juices to the air and starting fermentation. After that they were spread in the shade again, then rolled again – a number of times. All this while they were fermenting. At the right point of fermentation, *as judged by the smell*, they were put into a hot pan and roasted to kill them. More cooling, rolling, roasting completed the process. There were numerous modifications or varieties but it may be said that the Chinese process involved twelve separate operations and lasted for three days.

Ingenuity unhampered by thousand-year-old tradition has cut down the operations from twelve to six –withering, rolling, green-leaf sifting, fermentation, firing, grading – while machines have greatly reduced the labour and the time involved.

Withering machines were introduced by 1890, with fan-driven hot air. Rolling machines had come a decade earlier, replacing an army of labourers who could only handle 30 or 40 lb a day. Sifting, firing and grading machines were all in use by the end of the century. Only fermentation, being a natural process, had to be left to take its own time. In fact the modern tendency is to slow this down by providing cool conditions where quality tea is concerned, for high temperatures and hurry at this stage adversely affect the strength of the final liquor. But rolling and fermenting together only take about three hours. Withering, still a semi-natural process, takes between sixteen and twenty-four hours.

The purpose of the six operations is as follows. Withering is carried only to the stage where the leaves become flaccid and pliable for rolling. They lose from a quarter to a third of their weight by evaporation. Minor chemical changes take place. Tea can be made without withering – by cutting it into thin slices like tobacco – but the traditionalists at least consider that the result is not so good. Pulping has been tried instead of withering, rolling and fermenting – which at least saves labour.

Rolling breaks the cells and liberates the juices. They are exposed to the air and absorb oxygen. In fact oxidization might be a better word than fermentation. A significant chemical change is brought about. The essential oils which give tea its aroma are liberated. (This is what was meant by bringing out the essential characteristics.) One gets the impression that all the delicate odours which make up the aroma of tea rise one by one from the leaf while it is being treated. The identification of smells is part of the expert tea man's stock in trade, so I will quote the widely experienced authority, C. R. Harler:

'Freshly plucked tea-leaf has the same spicey smell as growing leaf, resembling that of ginger root or the concentrated smell of hay with the acrid part predominating As withering proceeds, the leaf develops a marked fruity smell, as of apples. During the first ten minutes or so of rolling the fruity smell is accentuated and includes the smell of pears, the last being strong when under-withered leaf is rolled.

'As the leaf ferments, the fruity smell fades, and a nutty aroma, as of almonds, together with the basic spicey smell, becomes apparent. With flowery teas the flower-like smell is also evident at this stage.

'Freshly fired tea has a smell of burnt toast and also a caramel smell of burnt sugar. . . .'

A cornucopia!

The leaves change colour during fermentation. And they are liable to infection, so scrupulous cleanliness is essential to avoid the risk of taints. The twist in the finished tea-leaf is caused during rolling.

Before moving on, a machine with a fearsome name must

be mentioned – the C.T.C. which stands for Crushing, Tearing, Curling. It is most effectively used on coarse leaf, and leaf plucked in the rains, which is far from refined. The rough treatment it gives the leaf makes it more susceptible to oxidization.

Fermentation has been described directly after rolling because rolling causes it to develop. But on its way from the rol'-r to the fermenting floor the leaf, already torn and twisted, ιs forced through sieves which ensure that all the pieces are less than a certain size. (If larger they would ferment too slowly.) This is green leaf sifting.

Firing is also called drying, and it takes place when the leaf with most of its moisture still in it is subjected to a blast of hot air. To ensure that the drying is through and through, not superficial, the heat is at first gentle and then progressively greater. But the other thing which takes place during firing is that the enzymes which were active during fermentation are inactivated. Also all bacteria ought to have been destroyed. The tea has been made – in the manufacturing sense. It is ready to be 'made' with boiling water in a pot.

It is perfectly drinkable, but most housewives would probably reject it, or take it back and complain, if it were offered to them in a shop. What remains to be done gives a hint of what will be described in the next chapter. This will be mainly concerned with the provision of a uniform *taste*. But the necessary preliminary – sorting at the time of manufacture – is done to segregate the different *sizes* and *shapes* of leaf fragment.

During the operation of green-leaf sifting, all the fragments were reduced to a certain maximum size. But all which were smaller than that passed through the sieve. And because fragments of differing sizes were variously affected by the different. processes of manufacture, and would give varying results in boiling water, they must all be segregated. The main division made is between leaf grades and broken grades, the former being the larger fragments. Leaf grades give a lighter coloured and less strong tea, and are favoured on the European continent. Broken grades, which yield a strong dark liquor are generally preferred in Britain (though not by the writer). Leaf grades are subdivided into Orange Pekoe, Pekoe and Pekoe

Souchong; broken grades into Broken Orange Pekoe, Broken Pekoe, Broken Pekoe Souchong, Fannings and Dust.

It must be noted, and kept in mind in spite of what you may formerly have believed, or been told to the contrary, that these gradings refer to size, appearance, and the facility with which the fragments are infused. They are not gradings of quality. In taste, Orange Pekoe can be less than Dust.

CHAPTER XI

Blending and Marketing

The poor only like to buy their tea where it is
brilliantly lighted and eloquently ticketed.

> *John Ruskin,* after an un-
> successful experiment in
> selling good tea to the
> poor of Paddington

THE main tea-producing countries of the world are China
(still much the biggest source though it exports very little to
the West nowadays), Japan, India (north, north-east and south),
Pakistan, Ceylon, Indonesia (Java and Sumatra) and Africa
(Kenya, Uganda, Congo, Tanganyika, Nyasaland, Portuguese
East Africa, Mauritius). The product of each has a national
characteristic, and each district within each country is also
individual. For instance, Assam is famous for its strength and
body. Darjeeling has a flavour of grapes – muscatel and raisin.
The tea from the Uva district of Ceylon is pungent while that
from the Dimbula side of the island is flowery . . . and so on.
But the flavour from each district is not constant throughout
the year or season. Spring teas are quite different from autumn
teas, dry-season teas from wet. There are about 6,000 tea
estates within the various tea-producing districts of the world.
The product of each is individual, differing even from an
estate only a mile away, just as vineyards do; and each varies
with the season, even with each flush and plucking. If there
has been any difference in manufacture that also modifies the
taste.

Tea can have an almost infinite variety of flavours. If it were sold direct from the factory of the tea-garden to the housewife she might get a very good brew – as good as the cup which Robert Fortune drank in the Bohea Hills – or she might get an indifferent one. It would be a lucky dip. Without tasting it beforehand – which would present difficulties in the modern grocer's shop – she would have no idea what she was buying. And she likes to know. Even if bulked and mixed by districts or countries it would vary considerably with the season. But, in fact, when the modern housewife buys half a pound of tea she *does* know what she is getting if she has had the same brand before. Something significant has happened to the tea between the estate and the grocer's shop. It has been blended. This is an art depending on the educated gift of tasting. But to see the whole problem in perspective we must look at it historically.

When people bought coffee-house tea they drank what they were given. When, startled by a rap on the window, they bought smuggled tea they still had no choice. When they bought dry leaf from an apothecary or, later, from a tea grocer the choice was rarely of more than half a dozen sorts which bore little relation to the stock held six months previously. For this tea was imported by the East India Company and sold at one of its auctions which until 1784 were held in London twice a year and thereafter every quarter. For instance, a catalogue for 1785 lists only two Boheas, one Souchong with another to follow 'as soon after the sale of the above tea as they (the company) shall think fit', and one Hyson and one Singlo. There was very little choice in the days of John Company.

This was not primarily due to their monopoly but to that of the Hong, through whose merchants all tea had to be bought without any contact with the inland gardens or middlemen. After 1834 things were little bettered. Trade on our side was free but our merchants could still only obtain what China was prepared to get rid of. The Chinese monopoly was gradually ended by the growth of gardens elsewhere in the world. This happened very slowly – remember that in the 1860s the racing clippers were importing only China tea. Then people bought, if they could, the tea carried by the winning ship. If it was not the best it was the most romantic.

Gradually from the various districts of India, from Java, from Ceylon, later from Africa, a wider selection of teas – wider

Two leaves and a bud — the golden rule in tea plucking

Brand advertising in the 1890s

Co-operative advertising: Mr T. Pot

Uninhibited advertising, 1897,
captioned: 'A Royal Beverage.
"Mr President, may I offer you a
cup of pure tea from Ceylon
and India?"'

A French poster

both geographically and in season of manufacture, found their way to London and New York. Particular tastes could be catered for – and consistently satisfied by blending. Certain amateurs blended their own tea. They must have had great fun experimenting in the mixing – and boring their friends about it. But grocers generally did the blending, some becoming very skilful. They sold from the open chest, shovelling the weight required into the scales.

In a book of the early nineteenth century a tea grocer is thus quoted:

> 'The chests used to be spread out, and when his grandfather had mixed some of them together, *in the presence of his customers*, they used to taste the Tea; and the mixing was raised until it suited the palates of the purchasers. He further adds that whoever understands Tea, and clears home for example twenty chests of Hyson will find upon tasting them separately and accurately that some have too much flavour and are therefore coarse; some have too little flavour and are therefore weak; and that others have, perhaps, like those that are to drink them, some little peculiarity which proper union will totally remove. By making a judicious mixture out of these chests a better tea may be got than any of the chests taken singly could afford.'

Exciting chapters could be written about such specialists in the trade although their work scarcely took them from the towns where they were born. In 1725 Maria Tewk, a woman of thirty living in York, set up as a tea merchant. She was refused a licence to trade and fined for doing so without one. She paid the fine and went on trading. At last the Merchant Adventurers' Company gave up the unequal struggle and let her have her way. She founded a firm which remained in the same family for seven generations.

Unfortunately selling from the open chest was wide open to abuses. Grocers are no more alike than types of tea, and the bad ones mixed in smouch or mouldy leaf which had been left on their hands. And at his end the Chinaman – once the personal bond between John Company's buyers and the Hong merchants had been broken – dyed poorly coloured teas or otherwise adulterated them, most ingeniously. In any case selling tea from the chest made net weighing difficult, and a little bit of cheating very easy. Tea had to be wrapped in something to be weighed, and to weigh the paper separately and subtract it from the gross weight would have been finical.

> Just a little paper
> Weighed in with the Tea
> Makes a mighty income
> For a company.

At this point of history we are clearly approaching packet tea. It was in fact introduced by John Horniman in 1826 – sealed packets containing a guaranteed net weight of unadulterated tea. But before saying more about that we must clear up the problem of uniformity in taste.

Tea is tasted at every stage of its journey from the garden where it grew to the shop where it is sold. Tea-tasting and wine-tasting are basically the same in some particulars and interestingly different in others. Good tea-tasters make sound judges of wine. Both must have a delicate palate and an active olfactory nerve. Both must have used and not misused this gift and trained it for the job in hand. The brains of both, working with their superfine and carefully maintained instruments, register nuances of flavour and odour. They *analyse* them, whereas the ordinary brain working with ordinary instruments bulks taste and aroma together and merely records, 'I like it', or 'I don't'. There is nothing personal about professional tasting. The value recorded represents the worth on the public market, not to the private palate. To underline this point consider books: You read one and you like it or you don't, but the professional publishers' reader records what he believes would be public reaction, leaving his own tastes out.

So much for similarities between wine- and tea-tasting. A difference is that the wine-taster is concerned with estimating how the wine will last. Are its qualities such that it will improve or fall off? The old-time Chinese connoisseurs kept choice tea sealed up in jars for a year or two or three. But generally and commercially speaking tea is disposed of as soon as possible for with long storage it becomes flat. So the tea-taster analyses qualities from the point of view of their use in building up a particular set of flavours and smells – meaning taste and aroma – at a fixed cost.

What exactly are a taster's instruments? Palate is a misnomer for, in the mouth, one's tongue does most of the tasting. Its tip registers sweetness and its base bitterness. Saltiness is registered at the tip and on the sides of the front, sourness at the back edges. Strictly speaking astringency is not a taste but a sensation felt by the gums and the inner surface of the cheeks. Most important of all is the sense of smell. Liquor taken into the mouth reaches the olfactory nerve by the palate entrance. But inhaling through the nostrils is also useful when testing the aroma of infused leaves.

At a tasting session a large number of teas – several hundred in the course of the day – are tasted. A tenth of an ounce of dry leaf – the weight of a sixpenny piece – is infused for exactly six minutes (sometimes five) and decanted into a cup. The pot is then turned upside down and the used leaves piled in the lid. A sample of dry leaf is displayed beside them.

Picture a long room with a north light like a studio, for the accurate appreciation of colour is vital. The teas are arranged in column of three – at the back a row of tins containing several ounces of each tea in dry form, in the middle row the heaps of infused leaves, and in the front row the steaming cups. The dry leaf is examined visually to note the colour, twist, evenness of grade, presence or absence of dust and stalk; it is touched with the fingers to test crispness; then a little is placed in the palm of the hand, warmed and moistened with the breath and then inhaled. Then the infused leaf – the infusion as it is called – is examined. Ideally it should be as bright as a new penny and of that colour throughout. Often the taster makes a pile of the wet leaves and puts his nose into them to test the aroma. Eyes, nose and touch have already told him a lot about the tea. He is ready for the final evidence of actual tasting.

There is a certain dignity about wine-tasting. Serious men slowly chew the wine, forcing it into the recesses of the mouth, their eyes seemingly focused far away on the sunny vineyard where this wonder grew. Certainly the spit can be a shock but, done well, it is no more ugly than an exclamation mark accentuating the final judgement.

The tea-taster generally goes round with a spoon – quite a humble-looking spoon with none of the dignity of a silver *taste-vin*. He fills it with the liquor, as he calls liquid tea, and sucks this into his mouth with a noise very similar to that made by an emptying soda-water siphon. A second later – no more – the liquor is spurted out again into the big spittoon. Apart from the action being inelegant the tea does not seem to have been given a fair trial.

But it has, for the proof of the tasting is in the final blend. The violent inhalation of the liquor – it is more than imbibing – has thrown it against the pertinent parts of the mouth and up to the back of the nose for a final vote from the olfactory nerve. Tea-tasting is quick yet thorough, and there is neither bluff nor snobbery in it anywhere.

The judgement of taste is, I suppose, always comparative – a thing drunk or eaten is better or worse than a standard unconsciously set by the mind. Tea-tasting is consciously comparative. Tea is tasted in the factory of the estate as soon as it has been made to discover how it compares with the last plucking manufactured or some other standard.

An indent of tea – meaning a lot, in the auctioneer's sense – is sent to the country's market or export town. For India this is Calcutta, for Ceylons Colombo, Cochin for south India, Chittagong for Pakistan, Djakarta for Indonesia. There again it is tasted. It may also now be sold in any of those towns, by auction or by private treaty. But the auctions of Mincing Lane are the oldest and still the most important in the world, so we will follow it there.

It goes by ship, of course, but a sample probably precedes it by air mail and this is tasted in the owner's London office. When the bulk arrives it is stored in a bonded warehouse. It is inspected for damage, and the owner's selling broker bores holes in a few cases and draws samples from which he makes out a catalogue for the coming sale. The packers, the people who package the tea, are the prospective purchasers. They also take samples of the teas in which they have been interested by the catalogue descriptions. Having tasted them they decide which they definitely want and how much they are prepared to pay for them.

Tea-tasting has evolved a vocabulary which is exactly descriptive for those in the know. Thus dry tea may be described as 'clean', meaning free from fibre or dust, 'bold' if it contains oversize fragments for its grade, or 'blistered' if it has been too rapidly dried and is therefore swollen and hollow. The infused leaf may be 'bright', which it should be, or 'dull' or 'uneven' which it should not. The liquor may be 'brisk', 'flat', 'fruity', 'hard', 'pungent' – or describable by one of a dozen other significant words. In general it may be 'bakey', meaning highly fired, 'gone-off', 'malty', 'mushy', 'sweaty', 'smokey', or 'weedy' which is a very rude word. There are something like a hundred such specialized terms but recent tendency has been to cut down the vocabulary.

The auctions are held three times a week at Plantation House, Mincing Lane. By the time tea is put up for sale there everyone concerned knows all he needs to about it. The owners have selling brokers who supply the auctioneer. Buying is done by buying brokers who may act for several buyers, a practice which conceals the actual purchaser. The auctions are swift and quiet affairs. Everyone knows everybody in the trade, and the outsider finds the proceedings hard to follow. Each lot – thirty or forty chests of 110 lb each – is very briefly and un-emotionally described, bid for and knocked down to a buyer within twenty seconds or less.

So it passes to the packers. The main firms in Britain are Brooke Bond, Lyons and Typhoo. They do not buy a lot of tea to re-sell it just as it is, but to be a constituent of one of their blends. The blend must be standard in appearance, taste, body, strength, aroma, colour. The blender tastes and tastes, adding a little of this or that tea and tasting each experimental mixture against a cup of the standard blend until he has made up something indistinguishable from it. That would be difficult enough in itself but the blender must meet two other requirements also. Larger grades take up more space to the half-pound than do small grades. They must be evened out to go into the standard packet. And the average price must work out the same. If some tea has been bought cheaply, more expensive tea can be added. For example, at Lyons I tasted a Darjeeling which costs in India, to the trade, 55s to 75s a pound. It was unforgettable. A little of that sort of thing goes into the blend to heighten quality. In all, twenty or thirty different teas, perhaps from two or three different lands, make up a blend.

The blender sends his formula over to the factory. There the quantities are multiplied up – a case for an ounce or whatever it may be. On the top floor of the factory the constituent teas are mixed in drums. The mixture is sieved and passed under magnets so that any extraneous matter may be withdrawn. It travels down by gravity to the packing machines – being tasted once or twice on the way to make sure nothing has gone wrong. A fraction more than the net weight goes into each packet, just to be on the safe side.

The tea is now ready to be sold to the public – and, to increase its sales, to be advertised. Occasionally tea is advertised as a whole in a 'Drink More Tea' campaign. More often it is advertised by brands. We all know something about that. If tea advertisers lived up to the standard set in 1660 by their first English copy-writer, Thomas Garway, they would lead the field. You remember: 'Tea – maketh the body active and lusty ... vanquisheth heavy dreams, easeth the brain and strengtheneth the memory ... whole nights may be spent in study without hurt to the body ... it assuageth griping of the guts. ...' Strong copy.

The propagandists faltered soon after, and descended to smugness. This appeared in the *London Gazette* of 13 December 1680:

'These are to give notice to persons of quality, that a small parcel of most excellent tea is by accident fallen into the hands of a private person, to be sold: But that none may be disappointed the lowest price is 30s a pound, and not any to be sold under a pound weight; for which they are desired to bring a convenient box. Inquire at Mr Tho. Eagles at the King's Head in St James's Market.'

It was still further weakened by a bargain offer. From the *Tatler*, 19 October 1710: 'Mr Favey's 16s Bohea tea, not much inferior in goodness to the best foreign Bohea tea is sold by himself at the Bell in Gracechurch Street.'

Towards the end of the century advertising was mainly done by the publication of instructive books. In 1785 one with a striking title was published: *The Tea Purchaser's Guide of the Lady and Gentlemen's Tea Table; Useful companion in the Knowledge and Choice of Teas. To which is added the art of mixing one Quality with Another as Practiced by A Tea Dealer*, by A. Friend of the Public who has been many years in the East India Company's service, particularly in their Tea Department, London. Published without mercenary views at One Shilling.

Another book, published in 1827, was entitled *Tsiology; a discourse on Tea*, and was described as 'An Account of that exotic of the East India Company'. In the United States tea advertising began at the start of the eighteenth century, 'Green and Ordinary' being offered by Zabdiel Boylston, an apothecary of Boston. Forty-three years after Boston had its Tea Party this appeared in the New York Press:

'Auction

'The cargo of Mr John Jacob Astor's ship *Beaver* arrived this past week with 2,500 chests of prime teas, produced last season from the best Bohea and Sung-po fields; the sale to be conducted by Mr John Hone, the Auctioneer, by open bidding, on Mr Astor's Wharf, foot of Liberty Street.'

The Japanese were first in coming out with something new and striking. This advertisement appeared in 1927, illustrated by pictures of men in white coats looking through microscopes.

'Scientists discover health-giving power in simple
Japan Tea.

'A precious food element, believed to be a safeguard against several common ailments found in our favourite drink – Japan green tea.

'For those who suffer from 'rheumatic' pains –

'For those who have a sallow complexion –

'For those who are "run down" and easily tired out –

'For many of us – there is deep interest in the recent startling discoveries about Japan tea. In pleasant cups of Japan green tea, scientists have found an invaluable food element, a wonderful health-giving property which is entirely absent from many of the foods we eat.

'It is now believed that countless men and women may be missing the joys of perfect health just because their three meals a day give them too little of this all important food element – Vitamin C.

Etc!'

In America the Bureau of Home Economics examined this claim, testing the vitamin value of Japanese green tea on guinea-pigs. After a three-months' feeding experiment it was announced that guinea-pigs 'do not naturally like tea'. That was the only positive result.

An American copy-writer went one better by claiming that there is a 'sex urge' in tea. As far as I know this was never tested on guinea-pigs.

Co-operative advertising was started in Ceylon in 1879 – very early in its tea career, and in 1886 the Government helped with an advance of Rs 5,000. In the next year the Planters' Association adopted the suggestion of using a voluntarily supported fund for publicizing the tea of the island. This, in effect, was the beginning of a 'Tea Cess', a fund for the benefit of the industry as a whole, subscribed to by individual concerns in proportion to their trading value. The modern Tea Cess, however, is compulsory.

India's co-operative publicity campaigns began at the Brussels Exhibition of 1888. At the instigation of the India Tea Association, a cess was inaugurated, and still exists. The subscription was at first a small one, amounting to no more than a twelfth part of a farthing for each pound of tea sold. It has been used in many different ways. Early Indian tea advertisements made less extravagant claims than did the Japanese examples quoted. There was a little snob appeal: 'At an afternoon affair my hostess served me the most delicious cup of tea I ever tasted ...' There followed phrases still in use: 'Purchase a packet of India Tea. It costs no more....'

In the United Kingdom a 'Buy British' tea campaign culminated in 1933 with 50,000 displays by grocers. The following year there began a campaign for better teas. There were three slogans: 'What you want is a cup of *good* tea', 'Tea at 11 a.m.', and 'Tea the *safe* pick-me-up'. This was when Mr T. Pot was born. Some may remember the picture of him sitting at a table with a lady and remarking jovially, 'Now we must make this a daily affair.' Co-operative advertising by no means precludes advertising by individual firms. Of this latter some people may remember examples from their childhood – 'Mazawattee Tea' all over railway stations; Maypole Tea, 'a perfect little Tease', with the picture of a coquettish young woman holding a cup out of reach of her admirer; 'Hornimans Pure Tea: A Right Royal Drink', with the Prince of Wales drinking it; 'Lipton's Tea' written large on the side of a bus.

Sir Thomas Lipton was the most wholehearted advertiser of them all. He entered into it with the same zest as he did into yacht racing, in that sport carrying on the tradition of the revenue cutters (not the smugglers!) and of the clipper ships. He was forty years old and already a millionaire from selling hams and cheeses when on the way to Australia his ship called at Ceylon and he had the idea of selling tea to the masses. He bought an estate – not nearly large enough to produce a quarter of the quantity of tea he later sold – and marketed good-looking, standardized packets, 'Direct from the tea-garden to the tea pot'. He used to the full every medium for advertising then available. There is a good story of him on a voyage to Ceylon. His ship ran aground in the Red Sea, and cargo was thrown overboard to lighten her. Most of the passengers were crowding round the lifeboats, but Sir Thomas was busy stencilling 'Drink Lipton's Tea' on anything that would float.

After that the happy faces and jingly tunes of TV advertising seem a little tame. But, one way or another, five hundred million pounds of tea are sold in Britain every year.

So much for marketing. But an outsider with no strings to pull or axe to grind – a mere reporter who tries to be objective – cannot end without remarking on something which has struck him strongly. Tea has been handled by all sorts of people in its history, but those who are now concerned with it maintain the highest standard of the merchant adventurers. Tea is a very gentlemanly trade.

CHAPTER XII

Hot, Sweet Tea

'I had not gone more than a few yards down
the hill when I saw stumbling towards me an
old merchant with his head split open ... He
was suffering from shock and was quite in-
capable of giving any clear statement until
he had drunk several cups of hot sweet tea.'

Major A. R. Tainsh

TEA in recent chapters has begun to look smug. But it still
shows its true character whenever there is trouble in the wind.
One saw that as the black clouds of the last war were piling
up and we started evening training on some aspect of defence
or first-aid. For strain and shock the prescription was hot
sweet tea. When war was drearily under way the famed exotic,
though still robed in pleasant associations, returned part-time
to its original role of medicine.

To wind up this book here is an incident of war concerning
tea and tea men.

In December 1941 the Japanese invaded Lower Burma and
began to sweep northwards. Strained to the limit on other
fronts, we could attempt little more than a delaying action.
On 20 February 1942, the partial evacuation of Rangoon was
begun. There was some hope – whether or not it was officially
shared – that the enemy would be held before they reached
the northern limits of the country. In that direction fled most
of the refugees. How could they be assisted in getting
through the mountainous jungle which formed the one-time
buffer state of Assam to reach safety in India?

The military had their hands more than full. Alone, the civil authorities were not capable of meeting a sudden and enormous demand on their services. Some other organization had to be found to give assistance. It existed, ready made and willing, in the Indian Tea Association.

At the beginning of the war the I.T.A. had given half its supervising staff to the armed forces. Those who remained were early called upon, with the coolies whom they knew how to lead, to assist in the construction of military roads into Assam. This work had not got far when the civilian exodus from Burma was threatened. Thereafter all available I.T.A. personnel, plus many of their number seconded back to the Association from the Forces, were given the task of meeting and succouring the refugees. They would build, supply and run such camps as were needed along the routes.

The I.T.A.'s Calcutta Committee nominated a Projects Sub-Committee which was in effect the High Command. This might have been handicapped by the fact that all I.T.A. personnel were engaged on a voluntary basis. But, to quote from Mr Geoffrey Tyson's most comprehensive account, *Forgotten Frontier*:

'This supreme general staff received such loyal and continuous co-operation from proprietary interests of all kinds that it was able from the beginning to issue directions to the Circle organizations to supply quotas of managers, labour, tools, transport, doctors, medical supplies and stores of all kinds at the right place and, in spite of all the hazards of transportation in Assam, at the right time. The maintenance of this labour, equivalent in numbers at its later strength to many military divisions, called for a supply organization which could not only procure foodstuffs and equipment quickly, but also insure their transportation over the badly congested lines of communication leading to Assam ... In the first place it was highly important to maintain the familiar British supervision to which the labour had been long accustomed. Secondly, each labour force had to be self-contained and supporting, bringing from its gardens medical units, camp builders, pay clerks, etc.'

The Army and Air Force co-operated, but Operation Refugee was Operation Tea. And tea has another claim. The greatest single obstacle was mud. Mud slowed down walking to a mile an hour and very often less. Frequently it made the carrying of heavy loads impossible and of light loads difficult.

The supply of food was a perpetual problem, and in any case many of the refugees were in so advanced a state of starvation and exhaustion that a first meal of solid food endangered their lives. But tea, being light, was always carried by the rescuers, and whenever a fire could be lit it was brewed. Alcohol, on the rare occasions when it was administered, proved a dangerous, even fatal stimulant. But hot, sweet tea saved lives again and again.

At the beginning of May about 40,000 men, women and children were besieging the airfield at Myitkyina in northern Burma. Most were Indians but a good many were of other nationalities. They were all hoping to be flown out by the American and British transports which were arriving empty and leaving for India packed to capacity – carrying seventy people when their official load was twenty. The Japanese army was reported to be close to Myitkyina and advancing rapidly.

On 6 May a Japanese plane flew over towing a red flag. Everybody dashed for cover. When after twenty minutes nothing had happened they returned to the transports. The transports were about to take off when Japanese planes reappeared and attacked with bombs and machine-gun fire. All but one of the transports were destroyed. Many people were killed or badly wounded. The rest scattered in panic, dropping their bundles. Few of them ever found these again.

That was the end of evacuation by air. The refugees in Myitkyina were in a terrible position. Many had lost everything except the clothes they stood up in. Since they had expected to be flown out these clothes were their best – in terms of cost and fashion. Later on women were found dead in the mud in silk dresses. The women's bundles contained jewels and objects of sentimental, not practical, value. The men had papers and money. Thus ill-equipped they had to face a mountain march of well over 200 miles. But their chief disadvantage was psychological. Reaching Myitkyina they had believed their troubles were over. Instead they were only beginning.

Most of these dazed and frightened people followed each other along the old opium trail up the Hukawng Valley to the Pangsau Pass (if they got as far) and down to what became known as the Tea Pot Pub, the planters' headquarters at Lekhapani near Margherita.

Now let us look at it from India: until the end of April a number of planters with a coolie corps under their command were working up from Margherita and Lekhapani, cutting a jeep road for the military. When news of the impending refugee invasion was received this work was immediately switched to stocking camps with food and medicine as far forward as possible. The farthest limit reached was Namlip Camp, eighty-five miles from Lekhapani. But later, when the track became congested and muddy, this could not be maintained, for the coolies could scarcely carry enough food for themselves for that distance. Beyond that they would have become a liability, eating more than they carried. Directly this was realized air drops of food at the forward camps were rapidly arranged. These were all the preparations that could be made for the approaching refugees.

The refugees, for some reason believing they had only about eighty miles to walk, set off from Myitkyina with such food (very little) as they had been able to collect. For the first one hundred and two miles they had something of a road. Then began one hundred and twenty miles of mountain track, with I.T.A. food stores only on the last eighty-five miles, and later less.

On 9 May the wet monsoon broke. It rained without stopping for ten days, and thereafter there were only short breaks in the eternal downpour. The first result of the rain was that anopheles mosquitoes rose in clouds from the jungle. After the ten days' incubation period, malaria appeared. Those with whom it took the cerebral form died within a few hours. Others lay down shivering in the wet, with the same final result. Some kept themselves staggering on through a world of hornets, butterflies, mosquitoes, sand flies, carnivorous flies and leeches. All the larger animals had left the steamy jungle, as they always do in the monsoon. Dysentery and septic sores were soon rife. Flies laid their eggs in the open sores of people too weak and spiritless to clean them out, and maggots thrived in the wounds.

A British commercial party from Mandalay had elephants with them. These carried a number of people over the Namyung river. But, farther on, the elephants damaged the track to such an extent that it became a line of waist-deep mud holes.

Those who sank into them were often unable to get out again. Those who stumbled and fell face downwards in the mud several times were so demoralized that they gave up trying. The stink of death was everywhere, and the sight of it in its ugliest attitudes. Corpses lay contorted, their knees up to their chests. These were probably people who, unable to light fires in the wet, had eaten raw rice which had scoured out their intestines. Hovering about every corpse there were always brilliantly coloured butterflies.

What of the food dropped by aircraft? Some was found and used as intended, some was lost in the jungle, and a considerable quantity was cornered by a group of well-armed sepoys who sold it at black market prices to starving refugees.

So far it is all ugly, but we have been describing the part of the trail beyond the reach of the I.T.A. Within their range – the last sixty to eighty miles or so where the refugees were at the limit of endurance – the story might have been uglier still. Instead it is lit by touches of humanity, of heroism, even of humour.

My main authority is the diary of Major A. R. Tainsh, a Regular Army officer seconded to assist in the evacuation. Since he was outside the I.T.A. his account is unbiased. He published this diary, unadorned, as *. . . and some fell by the wayside*. It is strong meat, not for the squeamish. But it is the most realistic and vivid description of humanity *in extremis* that I have ever read.

He went forward to a dropping area where armed Punjabi soldiers were trying to build up a black market supply. He searched for the food bags with them.

'When we found one bag I ordered one of them to carry it out of the jungle to the path. I turned to go on with the search, and when next I saw this soldier he was in the act of tearing off the outer covers of the rice bag. I shouted to him to carry it up to the road at once where he would get his share. Instead he dropped the bag and swung his rifle at my stomach. It was what I had expected so I hit him on the side of the neck with a heavy rattan cane, whereupon he dropped his rifle, and as he stopped to pick it up I gave him an upper cut which removed all further desire to try any more mischief. On recovering he was quite ready to carry bags of food to the top of the hill and later in the afternoon came and apologized and said it was the first time in three months he had received an order from an officer. That evening he was served with a cooked meal and hot tea.'

For some time Tainsh worked in close co-operation with a tea-planter named Mackie. They got to know each other so well that no explanations were necessary. On one occasion Mackie went off up the road alone, pretending he was on some minor errand. 'It was typical of a planter to go off quietly, do a tough and dangerous job of work and see to it that if things went wrong his friend would not be embarrassed ... Mackie could look after himself, and being a dour Scot the jungle ghosts would not disturb him.'

The jungle was full of ghosts, or at any rate of unburied dead. More than half of those who died were young men between seventeen and twenty-seven years old. Men over forty also died in large numbers. Between twenty-seven and forty they were much more resistant. But the most striking fact is that only about ten per cent of all the dead were women. Pregnant women had the greatest stamina of all. Not more than two are known to have died.

They had the strongest will to go on living. Even with others, if the will remained something generally could be done.

'Davis was in a bad way. His legs were three times their normal size, due to very bad oedema. He also had deep ulcers all over his legs and huge holes at the back of his knees. His general condition was bad and his arms and legs were almost paralysed. Archibald came over and we discussed what we should do with him. The Garo porters refused to carry him down the clay side to Pateri Camp. The hill was too steep for the bullock to carry him. If Davis had remained up in Nanki overnight he would have died of pneumonia. . . .

'I put Davis on my back and tied him on with a dhoti and carried him a few steps at a time to Pateri. It was a painful business for Davis; his ulcers gave him hell, but I was too tired to worry about his pain. After three hours of stumbling about in the mud, and many falls, we reached the tea-stop where Peter Barnside gave Davis some hot tea.'

If the body was sound and only the will failed – as it was apt to do from the discouragement of weariness, strain and endless discomfort – then also help could be given. But not by offering sympathy! That is the worst possible thing for a person who is sorry for himself – it only makes him more so. Tea with sugar but without sympathy is the recipe. Revive the body and waken a spark of something in the mind – anger for choice – and the patient is half-way to recovery.

'Further on we found a family who had spent a night huddled under a sheet. Our shouts and yells did not cause them to stir, so I pulled off the sheet and found a father, mother and son all crouched under it with their heads resting on their knees. They refused to move and tried to pull the sheet back. The father said they were tired of the struggle of trying to reach India and were going to stay there and die. I had some sweet tea in my flask and gave each a drink and some biscuits. We told them to get moving but they had not the mental energy to make the attempt. I pulled the child on to his feet but he just sat down again – he was cold and stiff. We then pulled up the father and mother but the same thing happened. It was easier to die than reach India. However, we were determined that all who could be saved should reach the base. We shouted and yelled at them, and then started to beat them lightly on the arms, legs and body. This stimulated them sufficiently to make them get up; a little more physical encouragement and they were shuffling down the road. We made them as angry as we could, and handed them another biscuit each, threatening a real good hiding if we had to come out and search for them in the morning. All the way along the road we found groups of people who wanted to remain behind and die, but we made it so hot for them that they found it more pleasant to keep ahead of us.'

Tainsh, as one gets to know him from his diary, is not one to hand out empty compliments. But summing up his experiences he says:

'The task of bringing these thousands of refugees to safety could not have been accomplished without the untiring co-operation and organization of men of far-reaching vision, engineering skill, medical knowledge and familiarity with local conditions in face of many horrors, hardships and set-backs. All this, and much more besides, was given willingly and joyfully by a team who had worked together for many years under the proud title of the India Tea Association.'

194

In peace-time tea is no less important than it was in war. More than any other food or beverage it has changed our way of life and national history. The story which began in China so long ago still continues, grows, develops. What a lot of past significance is in the quietly steaming cup, and what of the future might we know if we could read the leaves! As for the present – very seldom do we go through a day without drinking, thinking, reading or hearing about tea. And that is true of almost every country in the world whatever may be the race, creed, or politics of its inhabitants. Tea is in the office and the factory, the train, the aeroplane. It is on the high mountains, in the bush or forest, on the sea and under it. It is drunk from eggshell cups of translucent porcelain and mugs of earthenware; from the most expensive china, from a cup of jade in a golden saucer such as was offered to Père Huc, and from chipped old military mugs. It is in the palace, the country house, the suburban semi-detached and the cottage of the labourer. Essentially, classlessly, it belongs to every home. It is the form of hospitality which can be offered by the rich to the poor or the poor to the rich, equally and without embarrassment on either side. It celebrates domestic happiness and soothes the nerves of failure or fatigue. It is the drink of conference and hearthside discussion. In James Hurnard's lines:

> Every good cause and every generous object
> Gains strength, and purpose, and determination
> When it is heated over a cup of tea.

The object of this book has been to help people to appreciate the world's cheapest luxury by knowing more of its history.

Bibliography

ANTROBUS, H. A.: *A History of the Assam Company* (Edinburgh: T. & A. Constable, 1957).

BAILDON, SAMUEL: *The Tea Industry in India* (London, W. H. Allen, 1882).

BALL, SAMUEL: *On the Cultivation of Tea in China* (London: Longman Brown and Green & Longman, 1848).

CAMPBELL, C. F.: *China Tea Clippers* (London, Adlard Coles, 1954).

CLARK, ARTHUR H.: *The Clipper Ship Era* (New York: Putnam, 1910).

COLLIS, MAURICE: *Foreign Mud* (New York: Knopf, 1947).

CROLE, DAVID: *Tea* (London: Crosby Lockwood, 1897).

EDEN, T.: *Tea* (New York: Wiley, 1958).

FORTUNE, ROBERT: *Visit to the Tea Districts of China* (London: John Murray, 1852).

FORTUNE, ROBERT: *Wanderings in China* (London: John Murray, 1843).

HARLER, C. R.: *The Culture and Marketing of Tea* (New York: Oxford University Press, 1956).

HUC & GABET: *Travels in Tartary, Thibet and China 1844-46* (London: George Routledge & Son, 1928).

HUNTER, W. C.: *The Fan Kwai at Canton* (London, Kegan & Paul, 1882).

HUXLEY, GERVAIS: *Talking of Tea* (London: Thames & Hudson, 1956).

KAKUZO, OKAKURA: *The Book of Tea* (London: G. P. Putnam, 1906).

KEBLE CHATTERTON, E.: *The Old East Indiamen* (London: Werner Laurie, 1914).

LUBBOCK, BASIL: *The China Clippers* (Boston: Lauriat, 1914).

LUBBOCK, BASIL: *Barlow's Journal* (London: Hurst & Blackett, 1934).

MACGREGOR, DAVID: *The Tea Clippers* (London: Percival Marshall, 1952).

MAXWELL WOOD, J.: *Smuggling in the Solway* (Dumfries: J. Maxwell, 1908).

MENNEL, ROBERT O.: *Tea: An Historical Sketch* (London: Effingham Wilson, 1926).

MONEY, EDWARD: *The Cultivation and Manufacture of Teas* (London: W. B. Whittingham, 1878).

MORSE, H. B.: *The International Relations of the Chinese Empire* (New York: Paragon Book Reprint Corp., 1910).

MUNDY, PETER: *Travels of Peter Mundy* (London: Hakluyt Society, 1919).

NASSAU LEES, W.: *The Cultivation of Tea in India* (London: William H. Allen, 1863).

RAMSDEN, A. R.: *Assam Planter* (London: John Gifford, 1945).

REPPLIER, AGNES: *To Think of Tea* (London: Jonathan Cape, 1933).

SCOBY, J. ROBERT: *A Revision of the Genus Camellia* (London: Royal Horticultural Society, 1958).

SHORE, H.: *Smuggling Days and Smuggling Ways* (London: Cassell, 1892).

TAINSH, A. R.: *... and some fell by the wayside* (Calcutta: Orient Longmans, 1948).

TEIGNMOUTH, LORD & HARPER, CHARLES G.: *The Smugglers* (New York: Doran, 1924).

TOOGOOD DOWNING, G.: *The Fan-Qui in China* (London: Henry Colburn, 1833).

TYSON, GEOFFREY: *Forgotten Frontier* (Calcutta: W. H. Targett, 1945).

UKERS, WILLIAM H.: *All About Tea* (New York: Tea and Coffee Trade Journal Co., 1935).

UKERS, WILLIAM H.: *The Romance of Tea* (New York: Alfred A. Knopf, 1936).

Index